ALCHEMY
OF THE
SOUL

Sarah Lahoski

Copyright © 2024 by Sarah Lahoski

Alchemy of the Soul

All rights reserved.
No part of this work may be used or reproduced, transmitted, stored, or used in any form or by any means graphic, electronic, or mechanical, including but not limited to photocopying, recording, scanning, digitizing, taping, Web distribution, information networks or information storage and retrieval systems, or in any manner whatsoever without prior written permission from the publisher.

In this world of digital information and rapidly-changing technology, some citations do not provide exact page numbers or credit the original source. We regret any errors, which are a result of the ease with which we consume information.

This book is for informational purposes only. By providing the information contained herein I am not diagnosing, treating, curing, mitigating, or preventing any type of disease or medical condition. Before beginning any type of natural, integrative, or conventional treatment regimen, it is advisable to seek the advice of a licensed healthcare professional.

Edited by Laurie Knight
Cover Design by: Kristina Edstrom

PEAK PRESS

An Imprint for GracePoint Publishing (www.GracePointPublishing.com)

GracePoint Matrix, LLC
624 S. Cascade Ave, Suite 201
Colorado Springs, CO 80903
www.GracePointMatrix.com
Email: Admin@GracePointMatrix.com

SAN # 991-6032

A Library of Congress Control Number has been requested and is pending.

ISBN: (Paperback) 978-1-961347-81-6
eISBN: 978-1-961347-82-3

Books may be purchased for educational, business, or sales promotional use.
For bulk order requests and price schedule contact:
Orders@GracePointPublishing.com

Table of Contents

Welcoming the Divine: A Prayer v
Opening to the Alchemy of My Soul 1
Trauma and How It Affects Us 7
Going into the Darkness: The Shadow Within.......................43
Beliefs and How They Affect Our Reality 61
Divine Feminine 75
Our Energetic System..83
Our Wise Soul Within 99
Finding our Golden Shadow: Our Light Within...................129
Tapping Your Inner Resources of Presence 145
Bringing the Light into the World 161
Reading List...167
Bibliography 169
About the Author 171

Welcoming the Divine: A Prayer

Divine Mother, please open my heart so that I may engage fully and unconditionally, reminding me of the boundless love you have for all of us.

Divine Mother, I humbly ask for your guidance to lead each step of my journey with wisdom and truth.

Divine Mother, I am ready and willing to take the necessary steps to wholeheartedly embrace my authenticity and release all conditioning that no longer serves me.

I offer my deepest reverence to your infinite love, compassion, creativity, and unwavering truth.

Divine Father, I call upon your divine presence to clear my thoughts of any negativity and misuse of power.

Divine Father, I seek your assistance in grounding my steps as I navigate the world, approaching it with gentleness and grace.

I humbly request your support as I carry my teachings and serve the world, fostering unity and sharing universal truths.

Om, Amen

Opening to the Alchemy of My Soul

When I look back to my younger years before I went to school things seemed simple. Obviously as a toddler there are a few complexities to life. But this part of me still remembered my connection to God. I was always able to connect with my guides and angels. I understood that we were capable of great things and that what was thought possible could be so much more.

When I played in nature, I felt the spirit of our Earth, this wonderful place that holds us for our growth and expansion until we remember who we are. This time in my life was a strong footprint of my True Self. I may not have had the words for it, but I knew what it felt like. There was a sense of peace that no matter what happened it would be fine. I knew I would be held and guided to find my way.

I figured everyone could see what I could and felt the way I did. I did not think it strange to see things about individuals or the energy around them. I also knew it was not necessary to listen to what someone said but to watch their energy and see what was happening instead. This was the truth. The energy never lied. These moments were filled with such joy and love. It is hard to believe I would forget these things. How could I let go of the best parts of myself?

If I could go back to this part of me, I would tell her: Do not forget your truth. No matter what happens in your world you are never alone. You know how to do this, and you just need to tune inwards. All the answers are right inside of you. Remember your inner wisdom and divine expression. Remember your light. Stay in that space of connectedness with all the help you have.

But this is not what happened. Around the time I was five, we moved from this place and into a house that I knew was a horrible place to live. On the outside, the house looked just fine but, on the inside, it felt oppressive and dark. This move was a direct shift from where I had come from. This was no longer a place of peace, love, or compassion, it was a place that sucked the light right out of me. It wanted me to forget lightness, possibilities, and the truth of energy. It wanted me to believe I was these darker things.

Every family member changed in this house. Little by little, the light was drained out of us. At night I would hear the voices of the energies that had placed a curse on the land. How in the world at five was I to share this and get my parents to understand that this house was not a place we could stay in? Night after night I would lie in terror of these things. I started to believe that the only option to protect my light was to hide it. This was the point where I started to forget.

It was a confusing time. How could these things happen and what could I do with them? How could everyone change so drastically that I no longer recognized them anymore? Many nights I would crawl into my sister's bed to help me feel safer. My dreams became dark and full of terror. I started to act out and when at school was obsessed about what would be waiting for me when I got home.

No longer did I feel the peace and joy, instead I started to feel fear and dread. With this came patterns of coping that at the time helped a horrible situation but, over time, took me further and further from my truth.

This house is an example of what can happen to anyone. When we forget our light and truth, we move into the place of forgetting.

We move into the land of the shadows and forget what we truly are. We, instead, start to think from a place of fear and division.

This can happen for many reasons including loss of a loved one, divorce of parents, abuse within or outside of the home, being in a war-stricken area, losing a home, living with an addiction or someone with an addiction, and so forth. Each event that is difficult or traumatic, can dim the light, and we may forget who we are. The conditioning from these events wipes away what was once simple and very clear.

I have had session after session with clients in my transpersonal counseling practice using hypnotherapy who have wanted to remember their truth. Whether it is a desire to heal anxiety, depression, disconnection, noncommittal behaviors, anxiety, or traumas, they are ready to have a different life experience.

I have seen within myself and others a shift that if taken could change everything. But how do we make this shift? Talk therapy is very limited and only deals with the mental and emotional portions of the individual leaving the physical, spiritual, or even other lifetime experiences unaddressed or even acknowledged.

It can feel scary to commit to taking ownership of our life. Our systems want to keep things status quo—what is already known. Our ego wants to believe it is dealing with things just fine. We are conditioned, beginning with our parents and caregivers, to look to the outside world to tell us how things should be. There might be ways that families have dealt with things, and that may feel "normal and right" because it's "just how it is." Some families fight about issues, drink and make it go away, joke and deny, act as if everything is fine, control things, divide and side, explode in anger or rage, tell us to suck it up and quit being a baby, handle everything on their own without discussion, or any other number of ways of "coping."

When we are children, we need to go along with these things to survive. And just like in my house, over time we forget who we truly are. We forget to ask the inner questions or to even remember how we did this. We forget our creativity, zest for life, love for others, compassion, and Divine Truth. These patterns create deeper and deeper dysfunctions in our lives, often passed down for generations.

So, what is the point of this book? Good question. I want anyone who is looking for a different way of living to have it a little easier. I want our world to be a better place for future generations. It does not take the entire world to make evolutionary changes, but it does take our individual commitment to changing what footprint we leave behind.

Do not underestimate the power it can have when we decide to make a change to our internal landscape because when we are willing to look at our shadows and lower ego, we see how we affect our environment. We no longer lead by hate, division, and judgment, but we tend to hide these things about ourselves which is why talk therapy does not always work well. We need to access the unconscious in a different way.

So, what happens when we commit to healing and releasing our karma, traumas, and conditioning? We can then start to connect to the truth of who we are. We can start to release division and connect in a way that we would no longer want to inflict harm on others, whether through our comments, behaviors, and actions.

Sometimes individuals will state "WOW that seems like a lot to hold and do! I am not sure I can do that." But please know this is not about rescuing the world and holding other people's baggage or behaviors, this is about going inward and clearing your inner baggage—only what is yours. This is it. Nothing more.

At any time you are reading this book and feel overwhelmed, take a breath and remind yourself this is not about codependency where you must hold more than is yours. Remember you cannot fix things in others. It is the opposite of that. This is about being 100 percent responsible for yourself. Nothing more. It is about the ultimate in self-care which is not about going to someone for a massage, nails, or friends to have a drink with because that is not dealing with the issue at hand. This also is not about trying to fix everyone around you and convincing them they need to do it like you.

Yes, it can feel overwhelming. In the beginning, we realize we are responsible for the world we have created, and through this realization we must make deeper changes. But until we embrace this first concept, nothing can truly change. When we externalize our issues, nothing can change because we cannot make anyone do anything. That is up to them. When we make an internal shift, the external world will shift too.

From these shifts, we can then release what was never "us" to begin with because they were only created out of survival of our circumstances. Once we recognize and acknowledge that we are not who we have been conditioned to believe we are, we move from darkness (what we are not) and into Divine Light of our True Selves.

The world needs this now because there is a ripple effect when we step onto this path. Most of you who are reading this book are lightworkers and can feel on a cellular level that this is the time to take this step. It is time to understand that we too are creators of our world. We are being awakened into a different way of being and cannot bring our old ways. It is time we ask ourselves, what kind of world do we want?

If we look at history, we can see what we have created up to this point. We must make a shift and this shift is from looking outside of ourselves to see what needs to happen to looking inward to see what we have done. And to do this, we need to understand how. This book will do just that.

My desire is that we dream big. We must reach for the stars to connect as fully as we can to our True Selves. When this starts to happen, we will no longer have the urge to have wars, abuse, hate, division, and destruction. We can lift beyond duality into our Divine Mind and Divine Expression to create in a way that has not been explored yet. Each individual has their own unique fingerprint that cannot touch the world if it is stuck in the shadows, hidden behind conditioning.

We are currently experiencing and witnessing a balancing of energies. The wars, shootings, hate, and control can all change just by taking that first step into healing inner war, hate, judgment, and control. This changes our history, our present, and our future. Everyone benefits. Love creates more love, but it starts with self; if we cannot love ourselves, we cannot love others. If we do not believe in the idea of unity within (our inner children and shadows), we will not have it outside of us. As we heal and forgive, the world becomes a brighter and more loving place, and it starts right inside of us.

We learn to govern ourselves because we understand at a soul level that what we put into the world comes back to us. We become proficient at manifesting what we want. We experience and see what comes from our lower ego and learn how to shift this to our True Selves. We know it and we believe it; we trust it to be true and the landscape of our world shifts before our very eyes.

What will you see when you dissolve what was never you? How will that add to the collective landscape of the world?

Once we identify the illusions, we can tune into the higher truths and can create consciously. When we heal, we not only heal ourselves and our history, but we also add to the future generations of possibilities.

Take a moment and feel into what could be possible. What are you willing to release to embrace this? How will this change the landscape of your world? How different will your physical, emotional, mental, and spiritual bodies feel within?

Won't you join me in opening to the alchemy of your own soul?

Trauma and How It Affects Us

Within, there is a cracking apart. I must survive this. I do the best I can, yet I am never the same again. Please let there be a way to rebuild me back to what I once was! I plead for an answer yet from within this space it is so hard to hear a response. But I can come back from this, I must. I must remember who I was before this all happened.

Trauma and the Physiological Response

Often, there is a need to understand why we struggle with making changes in our lives. To discover the greatness within us, we must first comprehend what blocks us from reaching our full potential.

In this chapter, we will delve into our physiological systems and explore the factors that drive us into the shadows of our past selves. Without awareness of why we have made certain choices and how they impact our lives, we may believe there is no need for healing. However, once we grasp this understanding and recognize options that can better serve us, we become ready to embrace change.

Typically, when trauma is mentioned, we tend to think of significant (sometimes called big *T*) traumas—such as experiencing warfare, physical or sexual abuse, or the loss of a loved one in a traumatic or violent event like 9/11. Yet, there are also traumas in our lives that alter our responses to the environment. These traumas may not meet the criteria for post-traumatic stress disorder (PTSD) but are still considered traumatic. Everyone in the world has experienced some form of trauma, whether it's a breakup, the death of a loved one, or having to relocate to a new school and leave friends behind. Each of these traumatic experiences triggers an immediate reactive response in the moment. The brain's survival mechanism kicks in, urging us to choose the option that ensures our survival. This response tends to be black or white—either we take a certain action and survive, or we face potential demise.

This process occurs unconsciously and rapidly, as the system senses danger. Once this response is established, any similar event triggers an automatic repetition of the same response, also occurring unconsciously.

For instance, imagine someone receiving shocking news of a sudden death of a loved one. In that overwhelming moment, the system shuts down, numbing emotions. Subsequently, whenever the system perceives a potential devastating event or anticipates a loss, it instinctively shuts down.

This may manifest as a detachment from feelings and merely mentally navigating through life. It can manifest in relationships as an unwillingness to discuss issues, as the system fears potential loss. It might also result in attempts to exert mental control, aiming to minimize the pain of anticipated loss.

In that moment when the system shuts down, it is the only way it can cope with such a devastating loss. However, as time goes on, this mechanism becomes less efficient, possibly leading to complications in relationships. There is a perpetual lack of resolution, and it requires increasing amounts of energy. It's important to remember that much of this turmoil occurs beneath the surface. If you were to ask the person going through this experience, they might insist that they are fine. However, observing how they are functioning and interacting with their world would reveal a different story. This reactive response hinders connection, compassion, communication, and the authentic expression of their True Selves because they are trapped in survival mode.

We often rely on tools that are ill-equipped to handle such situations. The following chapters will discuss trauma, stress, post-traumatic stress, post-traumatic stress disorder, and a variety of approaches to overcoming trauma. Additionally, it will explore the physiological effects on our systems, encompassing brain responses, physical reactions, and the development of stuck patterns in individuals' lives.

The purpose of this exploration is to shed light on the fact that when we experience trauma, our ego, fearing its demise, seeks ways to ensure survival. However, this disconnects us from our higher resources that remind us of our vast capabilities beyond the traumatic experience. As we progress, it is essential to keep in mind that these effects may manifest unexpectedly in various aspects of life.

Trauma

According to Webster's dictionary, trauma is defined as an emotional upset or an agent, force, or mechanism that causes distress. When most people hear the term *trauma*, they often associate it with PTSD. However, as we can see, that is not always the case. Trauma can vary in its impact, affecting some individuals greatly while having little to no effect on others. Everyone experiences some stress following trauma, but not all traumatic events lead to post-traumatic stress as a disorder. And, consequently, trauma is quite subjective and therefore difficult to quantify. Karen Curry Parker often suggests that anything that takes us away from our authentic selves can be considered traumatic, and I find this definition quite compelling.

During moments of trauma, the internal system takes over to help cope with the experience. It could be something as seemingly minor as falling off a bike and getting hurt or as significant as losing a loved one or going through a divorce. Even though these events may not lead to a diagnosis of PTSD, they can still provoke behavioral changes in individuals. As we proceed through this chapter, we will delve deeper into understanding how these changes occur and explore the physiological aspects of brain chemistry and how they affect our functioning.

Post-Traumatic Stress Disorder

According to the DSM-5, post-traumatic stress disorder must meet the following criteria for a diagnosis to be made

1) An individual has had exposure to actual or threatened death, serious injury, or sexual violence in one or more of the following ways.
    a. Directly experiencing the traumatic event(s).
    b. Witnessing, in person, the event(s) as it occurred to others.
    c. Learning that the traumatic event(s) occurred to a close family member or close friend. In cases of actual or threatened death of a family member or friend, the event(s) must have been violent or accidental.
    d. Experiencing repeated or extreme exposure to aversive details of the traumatic event(s) (e.g., first responders collecting human remains; police officers repeatedly exposed to details of child abuse).
2) The individual must also have one of the following intrusion symptoms associated with the event(s), beginning after the event(s) occurred.
    a. Recurrent, involuntary, and intrusive distressing memories of the event.
    b. Recurrent distressing dreams in which the content or effect of the dream are related to the traumatic event.
    c. Dissociative reactions.
    d. Intense or prolonged psychological distress at exposure to internal or external cues which symbolize the traumatic event.
    e. Marked physiological reactions to internal and external cues that symbolize or resemble an aspect of the traumatic event(s).

3) Persistent avoidance of stimuli associated with the traumatic event(s), beginning after the traumatic event(s) occurred, as evidenced by one or both of the following:
   a. Avoidance of or efforts to avoid distressing memories, thoughts, or feelings about or closely associated with the traumatic event(s).
   b. Avoidance of or efforts to avoid external reminders (people, places, conversations, activities, objects, situations) that arouse distressing memories, thoughts, or feelings about or closely associated with that traumatic event(s).
4) Negative alterations in cognitions and mood associated with traumatic event(s) beginning or worsening after the traumatic event(s) occurred as evidenced by two or more of the following:
   a. Inability to remember an important aspect of the traumatic event(s) (typically due to dissociative amnesia and not to other factors such as head injury, alcohol, or drugs).
   b. Persistent and exaggerated negative beliefs or expectations about oneself, others, or the world.
   c. Persistent distorted cognitions about the cause or consequences of the traumatic event(s) that lead the individual to blame himself/herself or others.
   d. Persistent negative emotional state.
   e. Markedly diminished interest or participation in significant activities.
   f. Feelings of detachment or estrangement from others.
   g. Persistent inability to experience positive emotions.
5) Marked alterations in arousal and reactivity associated with the traumatic event(s) beginning or worsening after the traumatic event(s) occurred as evidenced by two or more of the following:

a. Irritable behavior and angry outbursts (with little provocation) typically expressed as verbal or physical aggression toward people or objects.
b. Reckless or self-destructive behavior.
c. Hypervigilance.
d. Exaggerated startled response.
e. Problems with concentration.
f. Sleep disturbances. (from *The Diagnostic and Statistical Manual of Mental Disorders* 5th ed.; DSM-5; American Psychiatric Association, 2013.)

As the above reads, there is quite a bit of difference between experiencing trauma and developing PTSD, yet our physiological response to the initial trauma is the same. As I move forward, I will continue to break down what happens to us during a traumatic event.

The Best Way Out Is to Pass Out

At the time of one particular distressing event, I had no understanding of trauma. The following example perfectly illustrates what occurs when we believe that there is no alternative but to "escape."

I was in boot camp, navigating it the best way I knew how—through humor. I didn't mind doing extra push-ups or runs because I believed it would make me stronger with each repetition. However, there was one thing I desperately wanted to avoid: others being punished for my behavior. We were given chits (a note/physical representation of so-called chances) during this time, and if I recall correctly, we had three of them. If all the chits were taken away, the entire unit would face consequences. I did my best to be cautious and prevent this from happening.

But one day, we were required to answer questions while standing by our foot lockers. These questions pertained to the chain of command and general orders. As they approached me, nervousness started to creep in. When I was asked a question, my mind went completely blank. I had nothing. Just a minute earlier, I had all the answers memorized, and in that moment, it seemed as if that knowledge had vanished into thin air.

The realization quickly dawned on me that if I didn't provide the answer, everyone would face punishment in the form of push-ups. At that instant, my brain registered the distress signals that something was gravely wrong, and the only option I had was to faint. Thankfully, it didn't come to that, but it was a close call. Out of nowhere, the answer surfaced, and they moved on (although they might have also moved on because I must have appeared completely pale and terrified).

This was an unforgettable experience. It marked the moment my body went into parasympathetic shock. This response had been encoded in my system as a way to react when faced with such dire circumstances. If I didn't know something, the best course of action was to shut down and retreat because it would ensure my protection. This unconscious response was programmed within me, and when triggered, it automatically manifested in that manner.

I'm certain many people can relate to this, especially when it comes to public speaking. There is an inherent fear of standing in front of an audience, where all eyes are on you, and you are expected to confidently hold that space and deliver your intended message. This fear can push individuals into a state of complete shutdown as their system instinctively tries to shield them from potential harm.

Peter Levine, who wrote *Waking the Tiger: Healing Trauma*, explains the physiological reaction to trauma. When someone has had something traumatic happen, there are three options for the system: flight, fight, or freeze.

He goes on to explain that, similar to animals, we humans possess the same responses. The distinction lies in our prefrontal cortex, which enables us to engage in higher-level cognitive processes within the brain. However, as humans and in cases of trauma, this may not always be advantageous.

Observing nature, he noted that when a tiger is about to attack another animal, the targeted animal must swiftly respond to survive. If escape is possible, it will exhibit a flight response. If flight is not an option, it may choose to fight and defend itself. If neither of these choices proves viable, the animal will freeze.

Ideally, if the predator loses interest, the targeted animal has a chance to survive. (In nature, animals are aware that consuming something that has died could be dangerous due to bacteria, so they may leave it untouched.) If you continue to observe this animal as it regains consciousness and the imminent danger has passed, you will notice it starting to shake uncontrollably. This shaking is part of the process through which they release the traumatic event.

As humans, we have the ability to override this response and tell our system that it is not the appropriate time to engage in the release of shaking. It might seem like a reasonable idea initially, but eventually, it becomes necessary to allow the body to go through the releasing process, but as humans, we have reasoned and rationalized to the extent that we have actually bypassed this instinctual failsafe, and perhaps to our detriment, have overridden an amazing wellness response. Failure to release the effects of the trauma leads the body and mind to believe that danger still persists long after the event has passed, triggering recurring freeze responses. Physical issues may develop depending on where the trauma is stored within the body.

I have witnessed this phenomenon in many clients who have experienced trauma but were unable to release it. Sometimes it emerges during hypnotherapy or in body-based therapy sessions like craniosacral therapy. The human body is truly remarkable. When it senses an opportunity, it begins to let go of the trauma, but many people don't know what is happening or how to handle such a release which may lead to confusion for the person experiencing such sensations.

Following a car accident I once had, I noticed my body shaking. Another driver had rear-ended me when the sun obstructed their vision. I didn't see them coming, and because I had no warning, this frightened me. I distinctly remember telling myself that I couldn't deal with the fear at that moment because I needed to figure out what needed to be done. Inadvertently, I overrode my body's inherent and perfectly programmed release of the trauma by doing what I had been programmed or conditioned to believe was "right" and socially acceptable. I immediately employed my prefrontal cortex to suppress my response, which could have potentially released what was necessary to avoid future complications, such as needing a neck fusion surgery.

Fast forward twenty-some years later, another incident occurred when my husband and son were involved in a car accident during the return from vacation. This time, I recognized that my system was in shock, and shortly after receiving the phone call, my body started to shake. The difference this time was that I allowed my body to shake.

Over the following few days, I experienced emotional responses to the event. Once again, I allowed these emotions to surface without judgment. After those few days, I no longer felt any remnants of the event within my body. This was because I had permitted my body to release what it needed to, without inhibition, and I was ready to move forward.

Once the process of releasing trauma begins, the individual's body may start to shake uncontrollably. This experience allows the body and mind to reset to a new state of equilibrium where individuals can tap into their gifts and talents more freely, as they are no longer expending energy to hold onto or to hide their trauma. They might notice an increase in energy levels, a reduction in pain, improved sleep, diminished anxiety or depression, and a decreased response to triggers that once affected them.

> On a side note, when someone seeks therapy of any sort, there is already a subtle communication occurring between the souls involved. This communication operates on a vibrational level, and typically, both parties are unaware of it unless they possess sensitivity, empathy, or intuition.
>
> As the souls connect, there is a mutual recognition of what the therapist can hold and facilitate within the healing process. This recognition leads to an exchange or agreement regarding the areas that can be addressed and worked on. Often, individuals might have a gut feeling that a particular therapist is the right fit for them. It is crucial to honor this response, as there may come a time when it is necessary to seek someone else's assistance in addressing different issues.

Regrettably, we live in a culture where such responses are often deemed inappropriate. Some of us may have come from families that frowned upon or prevented us from expressing strong emotions, perceiving them as a sign of weakness or defiance. We might have even internalized messages urging us to toughen up, pretend, and move on.

These powerful messages do not make us stronger; instead, they weaken us—mind, body, and spirit. When we fail to allow ourselves to process and heal from our traumas, those traumas begin to define our identities, and we operate at a lower level of consciousness.

If we remain hyperalert to our surroundings, our bodies continuously function in a heightened state through the sympathetic nervous system. This sets off a chain reaction. The adrenal glands urge us to stay alert, and the energy expenditure starts to impact our hormonal, digestive, and cardiovascular systems.

Some individuals may struggle to calm themselves enough to sleep or they may experience panic attacks without understanding the underlying reasons. Suddenly, they find themselves dealing with high blood pressure and low energy. These manifestations occur because we are not meant to be in a perpetual state of high alertness. This constant vigilance gradually breaks down our systems.

We would never expect our car to keep running smoothly without regular maintenance. We change the oil and conduct various checks to ensure it operates optimally. When a light comes on, we know the car needs attention, and if we want our transportation to continue to get us where we want to go, we take care of it. But we don't give our bodies the same respect. When we fail to process traumatic experiences, our bodies begin to send signals, indicating that something is wrong and requires attention before it becomes a more significant issue. We often ignore or dismiss these signals. We don't always look for the cause of the upset stomach or the heartburn, but instead reach for something to soothe and relieve the symptoms. Imagine if we treated our cars the same way.

If we ignore the body's signals and fail to process and release the trauma, it will embed itself within our physiological systems, waiting for resolution. It creates ongoing distress signals, indicating that something is amiss and needs repair. Once we listen to these signals and address the underlying issues, we can move forward without adverse effects on our system. However, if we ignore them, the problems will continue to escalate until, at times, it may be too late to reverse the damage.

Trauma and the Brain

When looking at how trauma impacts the body, it's important that the brain is also considered. I have often heard individuals who have experienced trauma, whether physical or sexual, question why they did not respond in a particular way during the abuse. They hold some sort of responsibility as the victim. There is often shame associated with the belief that if the event occurred and they did not fight off the abuser, then it was their fault and a sign of weakness. This is very hard for people to reconcile.

But consider this: in many cases of sexual assault, the perpetrator is physically larger and more powerful than the victim, right? Fighting back could potentially have put the victim in even greater danger. Therefore, the most effective survival strategy was to shut down their system, avoiding the experience of the abuse. This is not a conscious decision, but instead a physiological response. Fighting wouldn't work; there was no escape. The greatest chance for survival was to freeze. This response is connected to the parasympathetic system.

Now, let's delve into what exactly happens in the brain. According to Pat Ogden, "We have three levels of processing in our brain, considered the survival brain. The reptilian brain comprises the brainstem and cerebellum. Its primary function is to ensure our survival in any given situation, and due to its instinctual nature, it controls the autonomic functioning of our body, including heart rate, respiration, digestion, and body regulation" (Ogden 2015, 180).

Ogden further explains, "With a primary concern for physical survival, this brain is responsible for reflexes and instinctive responses to stress and trauma, ranging from the startle reflex to defensive responses such as crying for help, fleeing, freezing, and feigning death. It may also trigger other behaviors related to survival, such as competition, aggression, domination, or the compulsion to hoard resources. As the reptilian brain governs basic instinctive actions, it operates very quickly, much faster than the neocortex" (Ogden 2015, 180).

This part of our brain acts as our first responder in any given situation, ensuring our safety. It functions as a vigilant protector, utilizing our five senses and sometimes even a sixth sense to ensure our survival. Individuals with this tendency often find themselves constantly monitoring entryways to maintain a sense of safety.

The reptilian brain relies on past experiences to guide present actions. If a certain response has worked before, it will automatically prompt the same reaction. This is why talk therapy alone can fail to address these automatic responses. When triggered, the reptilian brain acts swiftly based on what has proven effective in the past. It is not something that can be talked through; it simply happens.

Now let's move on to the next part of the brain, which is the mammalian brain. This portion of the brain is primarily responsible for emotions. Ogden describes it as "the mammalian brain (also known as the emotional brain or limbic brain) located right in the center of the whole brain, connecting the reptilian brain and the neocortex. The mammalian brain interprets the world through emotions and oversees our emotional response to relationships and events" (Ogden 2015,179).

According to Ogden, there are various components or structures within the mammalian brain that allow us to subjectively experience emotions, form attachments with others, feel drawn to certain things or individuals, and retain emotional memories of our experiences. The thalamus, situated here, receives information from our senses, including potential threats or danger cues. The amygdala signals to us the need to be alert, defend ourselves, and protect. The hippocampus acts as the brain's secretary, storing important information and consolidating it into long-term memory. "The mammalian brain is vital for our relationships as it generates feelings that make us aware of how others' actions impact us," explains Ogden. When considering the mammalian brain, think of emotional processing (Ogden 2015, 180).

To illustrate, let's consider a child growing up in a household with an alcoholic parent. When we consider the interplay of the two lower brain regions, this is how they collaborate. Suppose the parent comes home from work and the child has learned from past experiences that when the parent slams their bag down, speaks harshly, or emits the smell of alcohol from their breath, an immediate response is required to ensure safety.

This process occurs rapidly and unconsciously. The reptilian brain signals survival and urges a response. The amygdala recognizes the danger cues and swiftly selects the strategies that have worked in the past. These strategies may include being good, becoming invisible, or adopting a comedic persona.

As this pattern persists, it becomes more deeply ingrained and dysfunctional. What was once a powerful survival mechanism in a specific situation starts to permeate every aspect of the child's life, causing disruptions because the system is trying to signal that something isn't quite right. For example, the same child that developed the comedic persona may, each time there is tension, unconsciously make jokes inappropriate to the situation (i.e., a teacher addresses the classroom about a serious issue like theft among the class or grief of a classmate).

Last, we have the neocortex, which is the final part of the brain. "The neocortex is divided into the left and right hemispheres, both of which play a role in almost all our activities," explains Ogden. The right hemisphere, more intuitive and well developed at birth, perceives the world in a holistic, big-picture manner. It is associated with creativity and artistry and processes information implicitly and symbolically in a nonlinear and intuitive way.

On the other hand, the left hemisphere, less developed at birth, adopts an increasingly rational perspective as it matures during childhood and young adulthood. It views the world in a logical manner and processes information explicitly, analytically, and linearly. The left hemisphere is also responsible for most of our language abilities.

According to Ogden in her 2014 work, the corpus callosum, a bundle of nerves connecting the two hemispheres, plays a crucial role in bridging the right and left hemispheres of the brain, facilitating communication, coordination, and the consolidation of information. The neocortex, which is responsible for executive functioning such as reasoning, planning, and problem-solving, does not fully develop until individuals reach around twenty-five years of age. However, when someone has experienced significant trauma in their life, they may spend most of their time functioning in the lower two portions of their brain.

This limited functioning prevents them from fully accessing the neocortex, where they can engage in top-down control and consciously regulate their emotions and bodily experiences, allowing them to make more deliberate choices based on the gathering and synthesis of information from all areas. As Ogden explains, when we begin to heal our trauma, we can start to regenerate the parts of our brain, such as the amygdala (responsible for regulating the autonomic endocrine systems which is responsible for fight, flight, and freeze responses), that may have atrophied due to overuse during our trauma response.

It is worth noting that individuals diagnosed with attention deficit disorder (ADD) or attention deficit hyperactivity disorder (ADHD) may exhibit symptoms that can be categorized based on the DSM-5 criteria but may actually stem from a trauma response. As individuals address and treat the underlying trauma, they often find that their inattention symptoms naturally resolve. As communities and society continue to understand and approach behavioral challenges from a trauma-informed perspective, greater attention will be given to trauma resolution through body-based therapies and hypnotherapy.

When working in a hypnotic state, individuals have the opportunity to identify triggers in their lives that are connected to emotions, which directly engage the mammalian brain. These emotions trigger automatic responses that individuals are typically unaware of. By activating the unconscious part of the brain through hypnosis, they can process the beliefs and behaviors they developed to survive, which are often characterized by black-and-white thinking.

Within this space, they can explore different options and choose healthier behaviors. This healing process positively impacts the brain and body. The hippocampus (mostly associated with memory) can then time stamp this new understanding, signaling to the mind and body that the event is over and no longer requires the same automatic response. This allows the individual to operate in the higher regions of the brain, specifically the neocortex.

This shift into the neocortex marks the beginning of a transformative journey in an individual's life. They can harness the previously trapped energy and thinking patterns for more positive purposes such as fostering creativity, experiencing happiness, attracting abundance, and cultivating healthier relationships.

Brian's First Loss in Life

Brian had a typical childhood. He loved playing with his friends and using his imagination to create exciting scenarios for them to act out. He was often found outdoors, eagerly climbing anything he could find. The following year, he was anxiously anticipating starting kindergarten.

One day after school, Brian's mom arrived to pick him up, which was unusual since his younger sister usually napped during that time. Brian didn't think much of it until he got into the car and immediately sensed that something was wrong with his mom. Her voice sounded distant as she spoke, and Brian's hands began to sweat, though he wasn't sure why.

His mom proceeded to deliver the news that something had happened. Brian's heart sank. He had never seen his mom in such a state and was unsure of what she was about to say. She continued, revealing that his beloved grandpa had suddenly passed away. It was an unexpected and unfamiliar experience for Brian. His grandpa held immense importance in his life. Now that he was gone, Brian wondered what life would be like and what it truly meant for someone to die. Where did his grandpa go?

In response to this event, Brian's system unconsciously decided to avoid feeling such pain again by distancing himself from others. This automatic and unconscious decision led him to disconnect from people to protect himself from the potential pain of their sudden departure. However, what Brian didn't realize was that this unconscious choice also stifled much of his creativity, as his creative spark was intricately connected to his emotions.

Fast forward to high school. Brian spots a beautiful girl whom he is eager to approach and talk to. However, he struggles with self-doubt, fearing that saying the wrong thing might cause her to reject him. Despite his insecurities, they manage to become friends. Their friendship grows deeper, and Brian eventually feels ready to ask her out.

She agrees, and they date exclusively for the following year. But one day, she approaches him and expresses her desire to break up. She believes it is best since they will be heading to college soon. Brian's heart sinks as he struggles to comprehend her decision. He loves her deeply—how could she be doing this? Overwhelmed, he feels a profound sense of loss and finds himself unable to articulate his feelings.

Brian sinks into a state of depression and finds it increasingly difficult to focus on school. He internalizes the belief that loving someone inevitably leads to losing them. Consequently, he becomes hesitant to form deep, open, and loving relationships. Instead, he becomes withdrawn and distant when he senses that things might become serious. Often, he chooses to break up with someone once he starts to develop deeper feelings.

As illustrated in this example, Brian's system has instinctively developed a protective mechanism to cope with the fear and anticipation of losing someone. When faced with the death of his grandfather at the age of five, he lacked the ability to comprehend why people leave and only knew that it would be intensely painful. In response, his system automatically shuts down to avoid becoming overwhelmed by emotions. Consequently, whenever similar situations arise, his system instinctively shuts down as a survival strategy.

Over time, Brian forgets what it feels like to experience joy in life and often finds himself feeling isolated. He expresses his desire for a meaningful relationship but acknowledges that he seems to sabotage it whenever it starts to become serious. He increasingly disconnects from his emotions and relies on his intellect to navigate challenging situations. The false belief underlying this pattern is that by avoiding feelings, he can shield himself from getting hurt.

Unfortunately, this approach comes at a significant cost. It has robbed Brian of his joy, connection, love, and creativity. He senses on some level that his life is not progressing in the right direction, but he struggles to understand how to make a change or why he is experiencing these challenges. Moreover, Brian grapples with difficulties in forming intimate relationships and often feels a sense of loneliness. While he may have a vague awareness of the reasons behind his struggles, it is only through releasing these unresolved emotions that he can begin to transform his life and free himself from their grip.

Polyvagal Theory

The polyvagal theory, developed by Stephen Porges, PhD, explores the science of connection, safety, and trust. It highlights our innate biological need for social engagement, which is vital for our survival as organisms.

To facilitate connection, co-regulation occurs within the autonomic nervous system, which consists of the sympathetic nervous system and the parasympathetic nervous system. The parasympathetic nervous system includes two branches: the ventral vagus and the dorsal vagus, which are part of the polyvagal system. The ventral vagus represents the system of safety and connection, where we experience calmness, relaxation, and the ability to connect with others. In anatomy class, it was often referred to as the "rest and digest" system. On the other hand, the dorsal vagus represents the system of immobilization, activated when there seems to be no way out of a traumatic situation, leading to the shutdown of the nervous system. This is what takes a person into the freeze/fawn state.

Stephen Porges states that "the vagal paradox brought us an understanding of the autonomic nervous system not as a balance system but as a predictable hierarchy." This means that the system functions in a predictable manner (Dana 2018, 4).

Neuroception, the detection without awareness, plays a crucial role in this hierarchy. According to Porges and fellow researchers, people are consistently scanning the environment, engaging all five senses, looking for signs of safety and danger. Though not conscious, the body may respond with feelings of unease, mistrust, and skepticism. It helps us detect clues of danger and safety, prompting corresponding actions. Deb Dana explains that "neuroception is appropriate for the situation, and the autonomic state will bring the energy necessary to effectively manage the experience" (Dana 2018, 35).

Within this hierarchy, different responses form pathways. When we feel safe, we operate from the ventral vagal system, allowing us to connect with others, engage in creative activities, self-regulate, and focus on conversations rather than external noises. Research by Keltner on the compassion nerve suggests that individuals with high vagal nerve activity tend to respond to stress with calmness, resilience, conflict resolution skills, cooperativeness, and better management of bereavement.

If a sense of danger arises, the sympathetic response activates. Deb Dana explains that this response involves "protection through movement, sacrificing social engagement for survival" (Dana 2018, 24). It triggers an adrenaline rush, sometimes making the person fidgety and vigilant, searching the environment for signs of danger. Friendly sounds may lose their focus, while sounds associated with danger, typically in lower and higher frequencies, may be misinterpreted as threats.

If the above responses do not resolve the danger, the person shifts into the dorsal vagal system. Deb Dana refers to this as the "scared to death response" and the path of last resort. In this state, the person starts to shut down, experiencing dissociation, numbness, coldness, shallow breathing, a slowed heart rate, and becoming difficult to reach. This response is rooted in our oldest survival mechanism.

Deb Dana explains that an autonomic nervous system shaped by trauma becomes a highly tuned surveillance system. These normal autonomic state shifts in response to everyday challenges are subtle for many people, and even in moments of significant state changes, there is enough resilience to return to a regulated state. However, for others, the movement along the continuum of autonomic response is more extreme, impacting their moment-to-moment capacity for regulation and relationship.

According to the polyvagal theory, there is regulation through relaxation and re-engagement, resembling a brake. The vagal brake rapidly engages and disengages to bring the system back to homeostasis. However, when the opportunity to exercise the vagal brake is missing, the ability to move between states is affected.

The ability to return the autonomic nervous system (ANS) to a state of homeostasis indicates resilience. It is a process that can be learned as individuals recognize that their system's response is not their story, but merely a response to past experiences.

By identifying what disrupts their ANS, individuals can learn to regulate the system. The ANS can be likened to a ladder, with the dorsal vagal response being low in energy. When in this response, individuals can activate the sympathetic nervous system (SNS) by engaging in activities like walking around, focusing on their breath, and assessing their safe environment. In moments of fight-or-flight response within the SNS, slowing down the breathing and practicing vagal exercises can help reset the ANS. Deb Dana suggests that noticing one's place on the autonomic ladder is crucial, as it allows individuals to turn toward their experience with curiosity and attentive listening.

Understanding how our system works can help release the shame associated with our automatic responses. Awareness of our position within the ANS empowers us to shift out of unhelpful states. This knowledge is utilized in trauma therapy to regulate the nervous system of individuals who have experienced significant trauma.

Betsy Goes Up and Down the Polyvagal Ladder

After a long and tumultuous divorce, Betsy realized that seeking the help of a counselor might be beneficial for navigating the next phase of her life. She has been feeling constantly tired and finds herself sleeping a lot. While she knows she needs to develop a long-term support plan for herself, the mere thought of it overwhelms her.

Betsy is a mother of two boys. She had been working as a teacher but decided to quit when she discovered she was going to be a mom. Over the years, she found immense joy in being a mother, and her children became the center of her life.

During the divorce, Betsy's husband lost his job and turned to alcohol as a means of coping with the stress of financial instability. Even after finding a new job as a pharmaceutical representative that required frequent travel and client dinners, he continued drinking and occasionally smoked marijuana, claiming it helped him relax and feel better.

Betsy asked her therapist why she behaved the way she did throughout this tumultuous period. It never seemed to make sense to her. When her husband was away, she would feel energized and excited about life, activating her social engagement system. However, upon his return, she would become angry and resent his presence, nitpicking everything he did. This marked a shift into the sympathetic system.

In response, her husband would yell back, blaming her for his drinking habits, accusing her of nagging him constantly. Betsy would then withdraw, becoming quiet with slumped shoulders, entering the dorsal system. Returning to a more activated state would require energy and involvement of the sympathetic system. A day later, she would find herself cleaning with determination, using this activity to ruminate on her husband's irritating behavior. This would bring her back up the polyvagal ladder, resulting in agitation and irritability.

The following day, when her husband left, Betsy found herself sitting on the back patio, feeling alive and vibrant once again. She was excited to have lunch with a girlfriend and looked forward to their special spaghetti dish. In this moment, she shifted out of the sympathetic system and into the social engagement system.

As we can see, this pattern remains in flux and can continue with various events throughout the day. It is important for us to develop awareness of our polyvagal system and recognize our current state. With this awareness, we can effectively shift our system to where it needs to be.

Engaging in this exercise should be approached with curiosity and without judgment. Our polyvagal system serves the purpose of helping us survive certain situations. However, it is important to be mindful of when we become stuck in one system for extended periods, as it can lead to problems in our lives.

Dissociation

Dissociation is the process by which a fragment of an individual's soul essence separates from the main body of consciousness. This separation often occurs during a particularly overwhelming traumatic event. The conscious mind is usually unaware of this dissociation.

Given what we have discussed about the brain's physiological responses to trauma, it is not difficult to understand why someone would disconnect and dissociate when they feel they have no other options. This response originates from the lower functioning of the brain and is an attempt to cope with a situation that feels too difficult to handle at the time.

In a way, dissociation serves as a protective mechanism, shielding the system from overwhelming experiences. This can manifest in various ways, as each individual is unique. However, the effects can lead to a sense of emptiness or feeling that something is missing within oneself. This creates a dissonance in identity and a strong urge to reclaim what has been lost.

Over time, this dissociation can compound and intensify. Initially, it may start as a small fragmenting, but gradually, the individual begins to feel emptier and more disconnected. This occurs because as each part splinters off and holds the trauma, it also retains the person's inherent gifts and abilities.

For instance, imagine a highly sensitive and intuitive child. This child deeply connects with others and feels this connection wherever they go. However, if they experience bullying at school, they may decide to suppress this sensitivity, believing they need to conform to fit in. In that moment, a part of their soul essence detaches, taking away their profound connection. Something else fills the void left behind, such as negative patterns, illness, foreign energies, or even feelings of depression, anxiety, or anger.

As time passes, this child grows further away from their authentic self, becoming increasingly confused about their true identity. While most individuals may not consciously know how to retrieve that lost soul part, they are often aware that something is amiss and seek help. In certain traditions, this process is known as soul retrieval, where the disconnected soul fragment is retrieved and reunited with its rightful place within the person, allowing them to come home to themselves.

Dissociated David

David was excited about his first sleepover. His friend Jacob was celebrating his birthday, and some of their friends were staying the night. This was a significant milestone for David, as he had only been able to spend the night at his grandparents' house before.

He was packed and ready to go, with a special gift for Jacob. It was a toy that Jacob had been talking about, and David couldn't wait to see his friend's reaction when he opened it. Finally, his mom called him, signaling that it was time to leave. David hurried to the car, filled with anticipation for what promised to be an amazing night.

Upon arrival, two other boys had also shown up. They all eagerly ran to the door. David overheard his mom asking Jacob's mom about the pickup time the next morning. Jacob's mom suggested around ten o'clock, which worked well. The boys played, enjoyed pizza and cake, and Jacob was thrilled when he opened David's gift. It truly felt like the perfect night.

They settled down to watch a movie and share some popcorn. Suddenly, Jacob's older brother entered the room with his friend Travis. Although Travis made David feel uneasy, he didn't pay much attention to it. They started watching the movie and playing with some toys.

Later that night, as David was sleeping, he became aware that he must have been the first one to doze off. To his discomfort, he realized that Travis was in the room and touching him inappropriately. The next thing David knew, he was observing the scene from the ceiling. Because from this detached perspective, he no longer needed to feel anything.

Feeling scared and unsure of what to do, David decided not to tell anyone about what had happened. As soon as Jacob's mom woke up in the morning, David asked her to call his mom and arrange for him to be picked up. From that point on, whenever something reminded David of that traumatic event, he would dissociate and mentally withdraw to a place where he felt safe.

This response is common among individuals who have experienced similar situations. When there is no escape and the person is unable to physically fight back, dissociation allows them to detach from their body and avoid the overwhelming sensations and emotions that would otherwise engulf them.

Unfortunately, over time, this can lead to difficulties in being present in one's life and recognizing what is appropriate for oneself. It's like handing over the reins of one's life to anyone who wants to take control. The individual often misses important cues that require their attention.

Once we develop awareness of these fragmented parts within ourselves, various therapeutic approaches can help integrate and heal these parts. This process of integration can be incredibly transformative and empowering for individuals on their healing journey.

Prenatal Trauma

Up to this point, we have focused on trauma that we can consciously remember, as memory of trauma is typically connected to language. However, when trauma occurs without words to describe the sensations or reflexive body responses, it becomes challenging for individuals to express or even be aware of why they feel the way they do.

There is a need for a bridge to facilitate communication between the unconscious and conscious aspects of ourselves. In cases where our language centers have not fully developed, trauma may be held in the form of sensations and reflexive body responses. As individuals grow older, these responses automatically manifest as behaviors aimed at preventing further damage.

While it has been taught that infants do not possess memory before the development of neurons in the cortex, other studies have shown that infants and mothers share a deep physical and emotional connection. On a physical level, the fetus is sensitive to the mother's emotions and physical conditions through chemical and hormonal changes in her body when she experiences strong emotions, pain, or pleasure. Therefore, if memory is not stored in the prefrontal cortex or neocortex, it must be stored elsewhere.

Further research has revealed that in utero, infants can record and recall experiences as early as the third trimester. Frank Doggett explains that the type of memory recorded corresponds to the fetus's brain development. The brain follows a sequential path of development, similar to the sequential series of life forms during fetal development.

Primitive and reactive centers of the brain, such as the limbic or reptilian brain (brainstem or lower brain), develop before more complex areas such as the hippocampus (in the middle brain) and the cortex (frontal lobe). Since the higher brain centers are not yet fully developed, the hippocampus and cortex lack the capacity to process disturbing or traumatic experiences. Consequently, memories encoded during early fetal or infantile stages are stored on a primitive, reflexive level.

These early memories are deeply and unconsciously encoded and profoundly influence our self-fulfilling beliefs through unconscious selective interpretation and reflexive emotional reactivity. For example, when a mother undergoes anesthesia during delivery, the infant begins to feel numb, and their first memory in life becomes associated with disconnecting and going numb. This response becomes automatic.

Another example of this pattern was something I personally experienced during my own birthing process. I became aware of this pattern only when I was in hypnotherapy training, and we were focusing on birth-related issues. I could sense that it would be an intense weekend for me because I had my defenses up, although I couldn't understand why.

As usual, the teaching began on Friday to prepare us for healing. This particular exercise was recreating the journey of my soul coming to this earthly plane. However, I unconsciously replicated a lifelong pattern. I adamantly refused to participate in the exercise, expressing my strong opposition by saying, "This is so stupid, there is no way in hell I am going to do this."

At that moment, I didn't realize that I was acting out a pattern that had been present throughout my entire life. The exercise symbolized how my soul descended into this earthly realm. As I started to energetically connect with the energy present, I made the decision not to come. I refused to travel down the fallopian tubes as the egg. I remained motionless, frozen in this pattern of shock. When my compassionate teacher offered to sit next to me, I immediately rejected the offer.

A profound sense of sorrow overwhelmed me as I questioned why God had abandoned me and wondered how I could return to that state. This pattern of "resistance to life" manifested in various ways throughout my life, including being three weeks overdue at birth.

From the moment my soul incarnated in this lifetime, I carried the absence of a part of my soul. This was the part that did not want to be here. Of course, I was unaware of this, but its impact permeated every aspect of my life without my conscious knowledge. I resisted forming connections out of fear of being abandoned, yet I was oblivious to the fact that I was the one causing the abandonment.

My sensitive side consistently received the unconscious message that I had done something wrong and that I would be abandoned and left to die at any moment. This false belief kept me trapped. Once, Archangel Gabriel appeared to me as a reminder that when volunteers were asked to come to Earth to help, I eagerly raised my hand and said, "Pick me, pick me!" However, this part of me was resistant to integrate when I felt the energy on the planet.

The difference it made to finally connect with this aspect of my soul, which genuinely desired to contribute and be present in this life, was extraordinary. It infused vitality and connection into every area of my existence. I am grateful I discovered this part during that transformative weekend. Otherwise, I would still be unconsciously driven by a desire for death, constantly seeking a way to return to God, even though God had always been within me. I was never abandoned; it was merely my erroneous belief that kept me disconnected.

This realization also brought awareness to the behaviors I engaged in to perpetuate this sense of separation. I could shift my responses to ones that fostered connection instead of building walls in my life. Healing these internal aspects allowed me to cultivate compassion for others who were going through similar experiences, and I also recognized that if we can identify it in others, we likely possess it ourselves.

COEX

A COEX, or "System of Condensed Experience," comprises memories with a similar theme or common elements that are accompanied by a strong emotional charge of the same quality (Grof 2012, 3). Each COEX carries a fundamental theme that permeates all layers of the individual's psyche. The theme of one COEX can vary significantly from another.

For instance, a "COEX related to anxiety will encompass any triggers that evoke anxious feelings, while another COEX might involve the energy of abuse and include entirely different experiences." Grof regards COEX systems as "fundamental organizing principles of the human psyche" (Grof 2012, 39) COEX plays a powerful role in shaping how individuals perceive the external world, themselves, and others. They can contribute to emotional and psychosomatic symptoms, relationship difficulties, and challenges in intimate connections.

Unless a COEX is unraveled and healed, it will continue to exert control over an individual's life, whether they are consciously aware of it or not. Often, the healing process resembles peeling back the layers of an onion. Individuals initially work with the outer layers in therapy to gradually delve into the deeper layers. During this time, they may wonder why similar issues keep arising in different forms. This recurrence is a sign that the client is successfully progressing through their COEX, shedding layers and addressing the reactions associated with it.

What Is Lurking in the Shadows?

Wouldn't it be wonderful if life were as simple as thinking and feeling something and knowing without a doubt that it is correct? However, we are far more complex than that. In the new age movement, there is often a desire to stay in a space of light and love, which is a beautiful aspiration. But what happens when our external environment constantly contradicts this ideal?

Why is it so challenging to hold onto love and light? When individuals experience overwhelming trauma that surpasses their ability to cope, they call upon their unconscious resources. For children, this manifests as a pretend world where they can become whatever they need to be. For adults, they create a persona or new identity. In essence, their True Self goes into a witness protection program.

This persona gradually takes control of their life. Just like in a witness protection program, a protector is needed to ensure the real individual remains hidden (the inner child). The bodyguard assumes the role of filtering everything because they must ensure there are no threats lurking.

Unfortunately, this bodyguard often misjudges what constitutes a threat because its detection system is outdated and fails to recognize when something is genuinely harmless. When a perceived threat arises, the bodyguard will go to great lengths to shield the inner part at any cost. This may lead to destructive behaviors such as substance abuse, depression, drinking, or anxiety. But in their mind, it is all for the sake of protection.

As a result, an individual's personality becomes complex, giving rise to archetypes or "mana" personalities. Archetypes represent specific aspects that exist within us, sometimes operating without our conscious awareness, such as the prostitute, judge, healer, rescuer, and so on. Collectively, archetypes are something we can all relate to in one way or another.

The mana personality embodies archetypal images of supernatural forces. According to Carl Jung, the mana personality is a powerful figure in the form of a hero, chief, magician, sorceress, medicine-man, ruler of men and spirits, and a friend of God. This personality is exceptionally clever. However, since it is merely a pretender to the throne, its facade can eventually crumble and fall apart, like any act on a stage.

These parts are not as wise as they try to portray themselves. Let's take the example of the mana personality known as "mother or father knows best." It seems appealing to be this individual, but when overwhelmed, this mana personality becomes unruly, abusive, and incapable of maintaining healthy boundaries with their child.

Another manifestation of the mana personality is the powerful judge who believes they know what is right in every situation. However, when others fail to comply with their expectations, they tend to turn into dictators imposing their rulings.

There is also the mana personality of the holy man. We often hear stories of modern-day gurus who succumb to the allure of lust, sex, money, and power. Carl Jung aptly states, "It is indeed hard to see how one can escape the sovereign power of the primordial images. I do not believe it can be escaped. Once identified, one can only shift one's attitude and save oneself from naively falling into an archetype and being forced to act a part at the expense of one's humanity" (Jung 1996, 389-390).

Today, society conditions us to conform to numerous archetypes without questioning them. These archetypes, or manas, have always existed and will continue to persist. However, it is our awareness and understanding of these archetypes that can change the way our behavior impacts our lives.

First, we need to become aware of the archetype we are embodying and how it functions. Is it aligned with our higher self or our lower, unhealed aspects filled with fear, anxiety, and shame? When we operate from our higher selves, the archetype expresses love and respect toward others. But when we operate from our lower selves, we project our unresolved issues onto others. We often point fingers at others without realizing that we should also examine ourselves and ask, "How am I engaging in the same behavior in my own life?"

When the mana archetype takes over, it is like an inflated ego proclaiming, "I am in charge now!" It can feel powerful, and one may choose to relish in this state. However, Jung warns that "possession by an archetype turns a man into a flat collective figure, a mask behind which he can no longer develop as a human being but becomes increasingly stunted" (Jung 1996, 389). We must be cautious not to fall victim to the dominant force of the mana personality, whether it manifests within ourselves or is projected onto others.

Eventually, the ego becomes less identified with the archetypes or their projections, leading to a shift where the mana personality adopts a new attitude that supersedes both the ego and the archetype. This can be seen as an upgrade to our internal GPS system. Jung suggests that the only defense against the overpowering influence of the mana personality is to fully confess our weakness in the face of the powers of the unconscious. By opposing no force to the unconscious, we avoid provoking its attack.

There is a delicate balance between the conscious and unconscious realms. Until the archetypes, such as the anima and animus, find harmony with the ego, they remain autonomous complexes that disrupt conscious control and act as true "disturbers of the peace."

The healing journey often takes us inward, into the depths of the unconscious. By understanding and finding balance within these realms, we can step into a place of genuine peace and love, rather than a mere performance.

This journey involves several essential steps. The first step is adopting the perspective that we are not victims in our lives. Establishing this foundation allows individuals to recognize their inner power to effect change. Without a solid understanding of this power, it becomes challenging to progress further in the expansion of consciousness.

The second step involves connecting with our shadow, also known as the persecutor. The shadow holds immense potential for deep healing. By delving into the unconscious realms, we can transform and renew ourselves. Once this journey begins, there is no turning back to the ignorance of the past. Once we gain knowledge, we cannot un-know it. However, exploring these darker places ultimately leads to a brighter and lighter awareness of who we are and what we can truly accomplish in life.

The third step leads us to connect with our anima/animus. According to Jung, the anima/animus represents the archetype wherein women carry masculine qualities (animus), and men carry feminine energy (anima). The anima/animus can manifest both positive and negative characteristics.

For instance, in men, the anima embodies feminine tendencies such as empathy, love, and creativity, but it can also include emotional instability or possessiveness. In women, the animus can manifest as strength, courage, or vitality, but it may also involve aggression, argumentativeness, or rigidity. The negative aspects represent the shadow side of the anima/animus.

Revealing this part of the psyche helps bring balance to the anima/animus within ourselves, which subsequently affects our external relationships. Cultural expectations of gender roles have often inflicted harm on our anima/animus. By stepping into this phase, we not only elevate our internal processing to a higher level but also release damaging expectations that affect society as a whole.

Individual self-healing contributes to collective healing. The final phase of this journey involves delving into the mana personalities. When the mana personalities find balance, the conscious and unconscious realms work together as a cohesive team, with no single part overpowering another in an insufficient manner of functioning.

Another way to view this process is that as we heal different aspects of ourselves, we upgrade the ego. In this space, we can embrace our true essence. The true essence is the divine spark within us that recognizes the interconnectedness of all beings and acknowledges that we are expressions of the divine. It compels us to honor and cherish one another, leading to profoundly different behaviors and attitudes.

Autonomous Complex

In the field of mental health, an example of an autonomous complex can be seen in dissociative identity disorder (DID), formerly known as multiple personality disorder. According to Carl Jung, a complex is a fragmented aspect of the personality, also referred to as a "splinter psyche," that is associated with an archetypal ally.

An autonomous complex is precisely what its name suggests: it operates independently from other parts of the individual's psyche. Essentially, this complex has gone rogue, and the original system is unable to control its behavior. The autonomous complex can assume various roles, ranging from impulsive acting out (such as engaging in risky sexual behavior or substance abuse) to extreme internal authority figures.

When this splitting occurs, an inner dialogue ensues with the voice of the ego complex. "The confrontation of these two positions generates a tension charged with energy and creates a living third thing... a living birth that leads to a new level of being, a new situation. The transcendent function manifests itself as a quality of conjoined opposites" (Jung 1916, 90).

As a result of this fragmentation, individuals often behave in ways that are not beneficial for the overall system. It brings about confusion regarding their identity in the world and who is truly in control, as this part functions independently.

This concept can also be connected to the trickster archetype, which is similar to an autonomous complex, representing an immature part that creates defensive distractions to divert attention away from painful aspects. Like a magician, it aims to prevent people from looking behind the curtain to see what is truly happening. Consequently, the trickster archetype has free rein to wreak havoc in an attempt to protect the system.

"When these two archetypes, the trickster and the transcendent function, are conjoined, the transcendent function manifests a new perspective with a novel way of presenting it, incorporating elements of surprise, humor, and irony. This alliance occurs when the trickster stops resisting, lets go of limited beliefs, and vows to 'fight no more forever'" (Handout from Welwood 1990. Heart Centered Hypnotherapy Training).

We all have splits within our psyche. When we surrender the fight and choose to heal, the inner wounded parts have an opportunity to experience love and compassion for the first time, as the trickster and autonomous complex step down and surrender for the greater good of the whole. When we are ready to relinquish old self-defeating habits, we can create self-affirming and loving beliefs, achieve success, and embrace new challenges and growth. This process often requires faith to take the leap and allow us the chance to soar to higher levels than we ever thought possible.

"Warriors are not what you think of as warriors. The warrior is not someone who fights because one has the right to take another life. The warrior, for us, is one who sacrifices himself for the good of others. His task is to take care of the elderly, the defenseless, those who cannot provide for themselves, and above all the children for all of humanity."
—Sitting Bull (1831-1890) Hunkpapa Lakota

Resetting the System

So, to summarize everything in a concise manner, we are capable of more than we realize. It takes courage to delve into understanding the reasons behind our actions, their origins, and their impact on our lives. This process often goes beyond mere conversation; we must learn to access deeper layers of ourselves to reset our responses.

When we bring heightened awareness to problematic situations, we can uncover faulty thoughts and beliefs that contribute to a reactive self, which seeks to protect our wounded inner child. As we have seen, this can create shifts within our nervous system, affecting us physically, emotionally, mentally, and spiritually. Once we become aware of these faulty thoughts, we can shift them toward more appropriate ones that align with our desired life. This enables us to tap into our deeper potential. With increased awareness, we can identify when our wounded parts are influencing our actions, making it easier to shift our consciousness to our True Self and manifest the life we desire. This is where affirmations hold the power to change our lives. For example, if we once believed we were unworthy of love, we can now adopt a new belief that affirms our worthiness and attracts unconditional love into our lives. Over time, this new belief becomes embedded in our system and radiates outwards, reflecting back to us in our lived experiences.

However, I want to caution against becoming overly fixated on the healing journey. While initially exploring our shadows is necessary for liberation, we should not confuse ourselves with the aspects we are working to heal. It's easy to become addicted to the healing process, but we must remember that we are ultimately a divine spark of God, here to share our unique gifts with the world. The ego is a temporary aspect that aids us in our current life experience; it does not define our true essence.

To conclude, here are some final thoughts to carry forward from this chapter:

1) "If I spot it, I got it." When triggered by someone else's behavior, it indicates that there is a similar behavior within ourselves. Take a moment to reflect on where you exhibit the same tendencies.

2) If we believe we are victims of our lives, we will remain in that state. Instead, we should strive to cultivate awareness and see how challenging situations can contribute to personal growth. Identify the steps needed to embrace growth and make positive changes.

By embracing these principles, we can embark on a transformative journey of self-discovery and empowerment.

Going into the Darkness: The Shadow Within

In the dark of the night, there is silence. A place where all seems to calm except the thoughts that keep drifting by as if in a loop. It is the wondering of what will be and how you can correct it before something worse happens and the love for a child that aches for the world to see them for who they are. Pleading in all the ways they know how. Remember who I am. Whether by the acting out or pushing back they call you forward, remember me, remember me. Yet due to the lostness inside themselves it does not matter what is offered to them. It is as if it never existed because they have discarded it inside themselves.

When I was little, I used to have a reoccurring nightmare that always followed the same pattern. It would begin in the middle of the night as I found myself descending the basement stairs, my bare feet feeling the coldness of the cement floor.

As I slowly made my way down the steps, fear and anxiety would grip me, anticipating what awaited me. Despite the trepidation, I never turned back but continued my descent into the darkness. When I reached the midpoint, the closet door in the basement would suddenly swing open, and something would reach out for me. Overwhelmed by this energy, I would abruptly wake up gasping for air, filled with fear that it had captured me.

This dream persisted for many years, repeatedly taking me back to those steps, knowing that the lurking presence in the closet would be waiting. It wasn't until years later, during a hypnotherapy session focused on this dream, that I discovered the symbolism behind it. As a child, I had metaphorically locked away a part of myself in that closet for protection, deeming it unsafe for that aspect to emerge. This hidden part of me held unique gifts that shaped my identity, but I believed they would be destroyed if exposed.

That energy represented a fragment of my soul, persistently reminding me that it patiently awaited my return. Thirty years had passed, and it remained patiently waiting for me. The basement served as the setting for this dream because it symbolized a space where I had hidden away that part of myself. My unconscious mind, through the dream, sought to remind me of who I truly was and where that part of me resided. Until I was ready to reclaim it, it felt as if it had never existed.

I had distanced myself from that part and rejected it because I no longer identified with it. It represented my creativity, the ability to connect and create in various ways. It was the essence of my authentic self. However, somewhere along my journey, I received a strong message that this aspect of me was not acceptable. At a young age, I internalized the belief that my creativity and sensitivity made others uncomfortable, leading me to hide it as a protective measure. If I had possessed the necessary resources at that time to support and nurture that young part of myself, perhaps I would have made different choices. Unfortunately, I grew up in an environment where visions and creative expression were met with discomfort, so I suppressed those aspects within myself.

As a result, a shadow part emerged. This disconnected and cold aspect disregarded emotions and moved through life with harshness, not only toward myself but also toward others.

As we mature, we begin to understand that much of the healing process involves letting go of our self-perceptions and embracing who we are truly meant to be. Reflecting on that dream, I am aware of the tremendous energy it took to keep that hidden part of myself suppressed, fearing its emergence.

This is the nature of the ego. It believes in its separation from the source and often lives in fear of expressing its True Self. Once I processed and understood the message behind that dream, the nightmares ceased. I noticed a surge in energy and a newfound peace within myself. I began to step out of the metaphorical closet as a highly intuitive and creative being, embracing my authentic self. This shift allowed others to feel more comfortable being themselves because my walls of protection had crumbled.

So, in this moment, take some time to reflect on your childhood. What were you like back then? What activities brought you joy? Did you immerse yourself in imaginative play, creating whole worlds and experiences? Did you have imaginary friends? Perhaps your memories from that time are hazy. Allow yourself to explore and reconnect with your inner child, for it may hold the key to rediscovering your true essence.

When we are young, we are unaware that simply being ourselves is enough. As we grow older, we begin to notice the world around us and observe the behavior of others. Without anyone explicitly telling us, we instinctively adapt and change our own behavior to achieve positive outcomes in our environment.

Perhaps we realize that being a "good girl" or a "good boy" gets us what we want, so we start sacrificing our own needs and desires. Or maybe we learn that the only way to gain attention is to mask our feelings with humor.

Bit by bit, we start concealing parts of ourselves, resulting in a growing sense of emptiness and the question, "Who am I?" Unfortunately, most families lack the tools to help us reclaim what we have lost, and so it slips away.

But what happens when we find ourselves in an environment tainted by violence and abuse? In such situations, we must hide even more of who we truly are. We rely on our sensitivity to scan the environment for signs of danger, constantly ensuring our own safety.

For instance, if our father is an alcoholic, we become hypervigilant, constantly assessing his mood to gauge our safety. Upon his arrival home, we immediately sense the energetic atmosphere, determining whether he is in a good mood, which signifies safety, or a bad mood, signaling the need to become as inconspicuous as possible to avoid confrontation.

Through these experiences, we gradually disconnect from our inherent greatness. We begin to hide and shield these vulnerable parts of ourselves, ultimately becoming more disconnected from our true essence. Instead, we identify with the protective masks we have developed to ensure our safety.

When we are taught to seek direction outside of ourselves, we gradually forget who we truly are and start living a life shaped by others' expectations. This can lead to profound disappointment and sadness because how can we ever discover what we truly want if we constantly rely on others to tell us what we should be doing?

Our inner light dims further as we conform to the desires of those around us. Conditioning and survival instincts push us to conform to the tribe for our own survival. Over the past two years, I have witnessed astonishing behaviors in individuals regarding politics and COVID. Everyone is looking outside themselves for answers. I have sat with people consumed by anxiety based solely on what they hear on television. Often, this anxiety is triggered by past experiences that may have no direct relevance to the current situation, but their belief in its perceived safety keeps them locked in fear.

There may be no truth to these external influences, yet when I encourage them to turn inward, they often revert back to what they have read or heard. It is an automatic response that disconnects them from their True Selves, leading to depression, anxiety, insomnia, and increased substance use.

This is precisely the moment to shift our focus inward and examine what needs to change in our lives. If we don't address the underlying trauma patterns, our perception of the world will always be colored by this lens of trauma. This understanding allows us to recognize our interconnectedness with others and discover our own truth, independent of the protective mechanisms we've developed.

What is the purpose of our soul in this lifetime? How can we connect with it if we are constantly consumed by anxiety, fear, and depression? These feelings are not our truth but indicators that something is amiss, signaling the need for a course correction.

Imagine if we let go of the expectations placed on us by others and turned inward to identify our true needs. How much lighter would we feel if we released the burden of carrying everyone else's energy? How would our lives improve if we redefined how we approached work and creation?

By embracing our authentic selves and cultivating self-awareness, we can bring about profound transformation and embark on a journey toward fulfillment and purpose.

We possess infinite possibilities for what we can achieve and accomplish, but before we can fully embrace them, we must understand our True Selves. We must be willing to confront and acknowledge the parts of ourselves that we have previously avoided.

At times, it may feel like we are sacrificing things, and in some cases, we truly are. However, we begin to realize that these are the things that no longer serve us. It never ceases to amaze me how we hold onto misery, unwilling to let go of our stories that only perpetuate further suffering. By clinging to them and resisting healing, we condemn ourselves to a lifetime of unhappiness.

Yet, if we can view these situations as opportunities for growth, learning, and experimenting with what we are creating, life takes on an entirely new dimension. It becomes a journey of expansion, positive creation, and personal development, rather than a life characterized by a belief that everyone is out to get us.

Everything in our world is a product of our own creation, and it all begins with a thought. If those thoughts remain in the depths of our unconscious, negative thought patterns will continue to shape our external reality. If we are not experiencing peace, happiness, passion, love, harmony, and creativity, it indicates that there are still faulty thoughts and behaviors operating within us. By tuning into our emotions, we gain guidance on the steps we need to take for growth and expansion. This journey does not revolve solely around experiencing positive emotions, but rather utilizing our emotions in a positive manner. For instance, when we experience the loss of a loved one and go through the grieving process, we have the choice to lean into the pain, allowing our emotions to surface and facilitating the healing process. This can lead to personal growth, deepened faith, and a greater understanding of ourselves. Conversely, if we choose to avoid the pain, we fall into the victim mentality and become stuck in the story of loss, life stagnates.

Hence, it is crucial that we consistently look within ourselves to work with and upgrade these faulty programs that hinder our growth. By transforming our thoughts and behaviors to align with higher consciousness, we can effectively bring about change in the world. With our energetic field resonating at a higher frequency, we can venture into the world with new ideas and ways of being, inspiring others to see the potential for transformation if they so choose.

I found myself contemplating why it is often challenging for individuals to turn inward and heal what no longer serves them. How did we, as a collective, become so lost in the world's darkness? During this period of reflection, I received several dreams that shed light on this matter, explaining the processes that unfold.

In one dream, I found myself in a home designated for "healing." However, some individuals were resorting to sex as a means of healing, though everything about it felt inherently wrong. Others in the room turned to substances. As I surveyed the surroundings, a dense, dark fog seemed to envelop everything. The more these behaviors persisted, the more their thoughts and actions severed their connection with their True Selves.

Initially, these options may appear enticing, but before long, the energy grows heavier and heavier. In the dream, there was a large circular window emanating a bright light. Although this light held the power to disperse the darkness, it was as if the individuals were oblivious to its presence.

In many ways, we are trapped in illusions, relying on outdated ideas and tools for our healing. These illusions can manifest through various means, such as using sex and drugs as depicted in the dream, or through our reliance on technology and work, distancing ourselves from the world. Rather than engaging in the necessary conversations and taking the essential steps to disrupt these illusions, we inadvertently sink deeper into negative patterns in our lives. However, the path to liberation and stepping into the healing light of Source has always been open to us, awaiting our call to embark on the journey of self-discovery and transformation.

The second dream took place in a building where individuals moved about in a trance-like state. No matter what I did to get their attention, it seemed as though they could not see or recognize me. My guides explained that in this vibrational state, breaking free becomes challenging due to its density. While manifestations may take longer to materialize in this energy, breaking out of it becomes equally arduous. Despite repeatedly urging them to look up and see the light, it was as if my words fell on deaf ears.

The first step toward the light must be taken by us. Free will dictates that we must make the conscious decision to embrace the light. This decision triggers the underlying patterns that sabotage our lives, but it also provides us with a starting point for healing and releasing them, thereby removing obstacles to positive transformation.

At times, we may express a desire to let go of certain aspects, but deep within our unconscious, resistance persists. Our unconscious believes that holding onto these patterns serves us better than letting go. Consequently, it may sabotage any healing opportunities that come our way. Yet, in these moments, we must not give up, for they signify our readiness to embark on deeper inner work.

During the same dream, my guides instructed me to shift my perspective and become one of those individuals. Although I remained aware of my true state, it required immense effort to focus on what I needed to attend to. I was told to recite the Lord's Prayer to help maintain focus, yet I found myself starting the prayer but struggling to remember the rest of the words. The difficulty in remembering mirrored the sensation of being disconnected and abandoned. It became challenging to connect with the light. Deep down, I knew that all I had to do was embrace the light that resided within me, but I needed to remember its presence.

The energy of the dream was palpable, resembling a profound, dark abyss where the light failed to penetrate. It revealed that when we succumb to addiction, allow lower thoughts to dictate our lives, and disconnect from our True Selves, we unwittingly confine ourselves within a self-imposed purgatory. The darkness desires this outcome, hoping we forget that we are beings of light. By yielding to the darkness, we forfeit our truth and lose sight of our divine nature. As God's children, we carry the light within us, and when we embody fear, anger, anxiety, or addiction, our light dims and we forget we have it.

In a way, it is similar to the shadow that fails to recognize its positive aspects, the golden shadow. This facet of our being encompasses our magnificence, including creativity, intuition, love, humor, harmony, compassionate response to adversity, humility, and more. The golden shadow comprehends our interconnectedness with others and Mother Earth. It wishes for everyone to embrace their authentic selves, understanding that there is no room for jealousy or greed.

Abundance exists for us all, as we are the creators of this planet, possessing immeasurable power. The golden shadow often becomes evident to others as something they admire. One may perceive all their flaws while remaining oblivious to their own magnificence, unaware that they have come to Earth to contribute something unique.

By releasing what does not align with our True Selves, we can embrace our authentic nature. This process does not entail becoming someone else or losing the positive aspects of our lives; rather, it is the complete opposite. We release afflictions such as depresssion, control, uncontrollable anger, vengefulness, rudeness, and so forth. I trust you understand the point. In the light, the shadow propels us toward a deeper understanding of our true essence.

We are releasing coping behaviors that were never *us* to begin with. These are lies that we tell ourselves and others. When I am working with individuals, the fear creeps in that they are going to lose everything they love as they go deeper into the work: their spouse, loved ones, and friends. As you can see this is trickster energy and the lie can feel very real. What better way to keep us trapped in the dark but to believe we will lose our light. The light penetrates the darkness.

As we look at that list if we were to lose them, we were never those things to begin with. Love is not control, abuse, angry, lazy, or withdrawn. So, rest assured I would not have done this myself if I were to have lost everything. I too had these fears at one point and of course it is always easier to look back and think *How silly*.

My husband and I always laugh when we think about how I was before I started doing this work. I was a hard and unpredictable person to be around. We both see how it has changed our lives for the better and at times more than we thought possible. And I know as we continue to move forward it will expand beyond where we are now.

Releasing the shadow can help us embrace our golden shadow. This creates a fuller and more expansive life but if it sounds like something that does not serve you, stop reading right now and continue having your love affair with misery. For the rest of us, let us move along.

As Marianne Williamson states, "Our deepest fear is not that we are inadequate. Our deepest fear is that we are powerful beyond measure. It is our light, not our darkness that most frightens us. We ask ourselves, who am I to be brilliant, gorgeous, talented, fabulous? Actually, who are you not to be? You are a child of God. You playing small does not serve the world. There is nothing enlightened about shrinking so that other people won't feel insecure around you. We are all meant to shine, as children do. We were born to make manifest the glory of God that is within us. It is not just in some of us; it is in everyone. And as we let our own light shine, we unconsciously give other people permission to do the same. As we are liberated from our own fear, our presence automatically liberates others."

Trickster Energy

The trickster energy seeks to deceive us and make us forget the truth of who we are. It wants us to believe that we are unworthy, noncommittal, judgmental, angry, and fearful. These lower expressions of ourselves are based on illusion or maya. When we buy into the illusion of life, the trickster has succeeded in diverting our attention, causing us to forget our true essence. This can lead us to believe that we are separate beings, and it can foster materialistic tendencies that prioritize personal gain over the greater good.

The trickster energy can bring suffering into our lives. By understanding these lower ways of being and how they manifest, we can become aware of where the truth lies. If we refuse to acknowledge their presence and influence in our lives, they will continue to dominate, perpetuating more suffering. Our thoughts have the power to shape our reality to such an extent that we may feel trapped in certain behaviors, unable to see an alternative path, much like the difficulty I experienced in turning toward the light in my dream.

The trickster can be likened to the image of a person with an angel on one shoulder and a devil on the other. If we are unaware of these energies, they can easily sway us in the wrong direction. The devil, the master of lies, can be as persuasive as the most skilled salesperson.

This energy is pervasive in our current environment. It saturates our television screens and permeates our everyday lives. Some actors in advertising embody it, and the political atmosphere is steeped in it. So how can we become more attuned to its presence in our own lives?

We must practice the art of noticing where illusions and maya surface. This practice should accompany us throughout our day. By keeping a record of where these manifestations appear most frequently and in what areas of our lives, we become equipped to resist being led astray from our true path and authentic self.

Consider the following example. When my eldest child was preparing to move out and embark on his own life, I experienced mixed emotions as a mother. While I understood that this was a natural progression, I still felt a tinge of sadness. One evening, as I was mopping the floors and shedding tears while reminiscing about raising him, my daughter chuckled and remarked on my emotional state. Her comment caught my attention.

As the night progressed, I decided to delve deeper into this emotional response. The following morning, during my meditation practice, I set the intention to uncover what I was missing regarding this event. I also asked for love to flow through all those involved to ensure the best possible outcome.

To my astonishment, upon concluding my meditation, I realized that I had been telling myself a lie, one that led me astray from the truth. This lie propagated the notion of separation and loss. However, the truth revealed that we are all interconnected with God, and therefore, never truly separate. It was my ego that sought suffering through this distorted narrative.

This realization immediately dissolved the lingering sadness I had been feeling. If I had not taken notice of what was happening, I would have remained ensnared in the trickster's web of lies.

Another example can be found in the realm of social media. If we were to tune in to a specific channel, it would present a convincing message supported by "statistics and research." If we were to believe this narrative, we might feel a sense of safety. Yet, even in this scenario, we can discern division and fear. In the current world we inhabit, with artificial intelligence capable of fabricating content for television and electronic devices, we must exercise greater caution.

Switching to a different channel, we encounter an opposing message that contradicts the previous one. Both messages may be illusory, but given our preexisting fear, we feel compelled to choose a side. This choice is likely driven by our desire to assuage our fears, even if both options are built on lies. It is crucial to recognize that anything stemming from fear originates from the lower ego and will not serve us.

In Russia, for instance, the message regarding the events in Ukraine would differ significantly, aiming to placate fears by presenting a narrative that all is well and for the best. Such a message would alleviate concerns about the severity of the situation.

But if we were to examine the news from a different perspective, we would encounter a contrasting message. This message might highlight the occurrence of dreadful events but reassure us that we are safe here, as long as we don't provoke Putin too much.

From both sides, these messages may appear valid, much like my contemplation of my son's departure. However, what would happen if we were to elevate our energy and seek guidance from a higher source? Would we discover that the trickster energy had deceived us, leading us to perceive things in a manner that promotes resolutions and problem-solving through light instead of fear?

By identifying the illusions present in our lives, we gain the ability to step back and adopt a different approach to creating in the world.

Surrendering

Surrendering can be an overwhelming concept. For many, it feels like relinquishing control, which can lead to a sense of impending doom. When I first encountered this idea, I naively believed it couldn't be that difficult. It's like reading something and thinking, "I've got this," only to realize upon implementation that it's not as easy as anticipated.

As I embraced surrender in moments when it was necessary, I confronted resistance and the fear of what would happen if I truly let go. Was it wise to release control? Would I lose what I already had?

I soon discovered that while the concept of surrender appeared simple, the actual process was a whole different experience. My greatest challenge in surrendering has been as a parent. Parenthood carries a sense of responsibility to provide the best possible future for my children. Society often reinforces the notion that parents are to blame for every action of their children.

But what happens when you have a child who requires more care than the average child? What if each child has their own purpose and karmic journey in this world? It's intriguing to consider that during our teenage years, we may still be grappling with lessons and karmic patterns, beyond the influence of hormonal changes.

One of my spiritual teachers once shared a profound insight: our children are not truly ours; they are unique individuals with their own purpose. It is an illusion to believe we can control anyone's actions against their will, as everyone possesses free will and choice.

Recently, I faced a significant lesson and choice regarding surrender. Most parents can relate: our children can be our vulnerability. One of the greatest fears as a parent is the thought of something happening to your child. I believed that by exhaustively exploring every option, treatment, and resource available, I could prevent things from spiraling out of control.

These actions provided a false sense of security because, ultimately, my child had the power to decide whether to embrace these options or not. Deep inside, a quiet voice reminded me that while those ideas held some validity, they were not the crux of the issue. I had been telling myself stories about them for years.

My child's struggles began at birth and were still unresolved, yet I clung to the hope that they would miraculously disappear. The search for a perfect solution became a never-ending quest. I questioned what I was doing wrong and how I was contributing to this situation. What needed to change?

I would stumble upon potential solutions, only to find they didn't make a significant impact. The struggles persisted. It was exhausting, but a part of me resisted surrendering to this narrative. Surrender felt synonymous with devastation, an option I refused to consider.

I toyed with the idea of surrender, but swiftly retreated as if I had never entertained it. Year after year, this pattern persisted. I pressed on tirelessly, hoping that at some point, a magic button, treatment, therapy, or some intervention would transform everything.

Like countless parents with children who have unique needs, the arrival of COVID-19 felt like a barrage of unforeseen challenges. Situations emerged that we could never have anticipated. How does one find proper care for a teenager who requires supervision to access education but is left alone because their parents must work to provide for the family? What happens when a pandemic disrupts the availability of teachers who are also concerned about their own safety? How does a child who struggles with structure cope when all semblance of routine disappears?

It felt like I was trapped in an unending marathon. No matter what I tried or how tirelessly I searched, the marathon continued. One weekend became a breaking point, where I simply couldn't bear any more. My husband and I were utterly exhausted. As tears streamed down my face while walking down the hallway, I attempted to seek support, only to find no one available to talk to. I tried calming my racing thoughts, but exhaustion and overwhelm had taken their toll.

Up until that point, we had mostly relied on ourselves for everything. There was no respite or relief, and in some ways, we had brought that upon ourselves. Perhaps it took all those years to finally bring me to the point of surrender, and it happened in that hallway.

In that moment, I felt empty, with nothing left to hold onto. I realized that the only option I had was to surrender to what was unfolding. I had to hand it over to a higher power. I wish I had reached this point sooner, but maybe this was the perfect time, as things often align in life. In that moment, I easily slipped into a space of surrender and clarity. I knew that by surrendering, I could move forward no matter where the journey led my child or me. I also understood that this process would continue to bring me to deeper levels of surrender, expanding my faith and trust.

During this time, I began to turn inward and seek the lessons to be learned from this experience. I won't claim that every step was easy, and I still have to choose surrender consciously. I also realized that I am here as my child's teacher, to guide him in being present in this world as his authentic self. There was a reason he chose me as his mother, and I needed to comprehend this on a soul level, rather than attempting to fix everything from an ego-driven perspective. My ego desired everything to be good, but that wasn't what was required in this situation.

A higher perspective was necessary, and I had to learn to connect in that way to find peace. I share this story because I believe that although not everyone has the exact same experience, the essence of surrender is universal for those who reach that point. It is in those moments when the ego says, "I will step aside and open myself to other possibilities because I have nothing left." Surrender then becomes a process of releasing everything we think we know and allowing infinite possibilities to enter. As Eckhart Tolle states, "surrender is the inner transition from resistance to acceptance, from no to yes."

We are living in unprecedented times, providing us with an opportunity to assess our lives and identify what is not working. It's a chance to delve into the darkness of our shadows, both individually and collectively, and ask ourselves, "Where do I need to surrender old beliefs and behaviors that no longer serve me?"

If given the chance to take that step, would we be willing to look within and heal our own contributions for the betterment of the entire collective? In that process, would we be open to hearing others' perspectives without feeling the need to engage in constant conflict to prove our point?

As a society, we have become addicted to trauma and discord. Even the media knows that love, peace, and harmony don't sell as well. So, how can we shift this reality and cultivate higher values to usher in a greater change?

Our government is crumbling, our schools are outdated and failing to meet the needs of children, and our healthcare system has become profit-oriented, forsaking its true purpose of healing. Imagine what would happen if a significant collective of individuals came together for just one day to find higher solutions to our pressing issues. What would the world be like? What if there was a call for peace to dissolve our discord and promote unity and expansion?

Surrendering our deeply ingrained beliefs that feel so right can be terrifying. The challenge lies in examining those beliefs to determine whether they are rooted in fear, unworthiness, anger, control, judgment, or superiority. If that's the case, they serve no one, including ourselves!

When we start to understand why we hold certain beliefs, where they originate from, and how they no longer serve us, we can release them. I have heard and witnessed the transformative power of this work, time and time again. Even my husband, who was initially resistant and skeptical, decided to give it a chance. He was amazed by its impact. He wondered what would happen if everyone in the world took the opportunity to do this inner work. How much more loving would our world be if we realized that our personal reality is not solely about others' issues but our own creation?

His assessment was accurate because there is liberation in realizing that everything we need is already within us. When we harness that power, transformative and positive changes occur in our lives. Couples often look to their partner as the cause of their issues, yet they chose their partner because it resonated with something they carried within themselves. The resolution cannot be achieved without examining how it triggers us and delving into its root. The answers inevitably lie within us. The very things that bother us about the other person are often reflections of something within ourselves that we have yet to acknowledge and embrace. We may believe that we left behind what we disliked in our family of origin when we got married, but unless we confront and address those issues, they remain beneath the surface, influencing our lives.

There is no singular path to reach this understanding. While I have taken a particular route, you may find another path equally as powerful. All roads lead to the same destination, a place where love and light reside. If we are willing to embark on that journey, we will discover and receive what is meant for us.

When we release expectations and the notion of how everyone should act or live their lives, our own path becomes lighter. Surrendering is a pathway to liberation from suffering. It is acknowledging that we are also willing to release the darkness that holds us back—feelings of unworthiness, unlovability, indecisiveness, and more. Instead, we embrace our true essence and let our voice shine in the light, allowing the vibrations of our authentic self to create positive change in the world. This task becomes effortless because what could be simpler than embracing our innate magnificence as souls here to share our gifts, wisdom, and love?

What beliefs are you ready to release?

What steps are you willing to take to bring about change in your inner world?

What will life be like once you have embraced this transformation?

Beliefs and How They Affect Our Reality

I hear an inner voice inside calling me to the Divine. It is low and present like the sun that is always there, radiating its warmth and love. Release what you believe to be you, so that you can become who you were always meant to be. Feel my warmth and allow it to grow. Just like the sun on a cloudy day I am always there. You just need to remember where I am. Right there inside of you all along. Within this realization, all that you thought you were released like a garment that no longer fits so you can wear the light that you are.

When I was a young child, I firmly believed that I was capable of extraordinary things. My little self had no limits or boundaries. As a parent now, I can only imagine what a handful I must have been.

One of the beliefs I held was that I could fly. If someone were to suggest that this belief was untrue, I wouldn't have recognized it as truth in my system. That belief was deeply ingrained in my toddler self, a memory from a time when I didn't possess this physical body that now defines me as Sarah.

I vividly recall a day when my dad was at the church preparing for Sunday's service. (You know what they say about a preacher's kids, right? Well, it's all true, ha-ha.) While he was in his office, I ventured into the nursery. The nursery had bookshelves filled with toys.

I convinced myself that if I could climb to the top of those bookshelves, I would be able to jump off and fly. So, with the fearlessness and unawareness typical of a young child, I climbed those bookshelves. I took a deep breath and leaped off.

My landing was far from a superhero's graceful descent. I landed in an unfortunate manner, realizing immediately that I had injured myself. I was afraid to confess the truth to my father, so I approached him, cradling my injured arm. He immediately recognized that I had broken it. Off to the hospital we went, and I spent the next eight weeks in a cast.

You would think that such an experience would have altered my belief, but I'm here to tell you it didn't!

Once the cast was finally removed, I resumed my normal activities. Once again, I found myself at the church while my mom attended choir practice and my dad prepared for services. My sister and I were running around, being a handful as usual. After my dad had finished scolding us and instructed us to stop misbehaving, we remained calm until he left the sanctuary.

As soon as he was gone, my sister said to me, "If you climb up on the pulpit, I'll catch you." Well, I thought to myself, *This is a great opportunity to test if I can fly.* I climbed up, prepared to jump, unaware that my sister had heard my dad's return and fled. Oblivious to her sudden absence, I proceeded with my jump, fully believing I could fly.

As you can probably guess, I broke my arm again. Same arm, same place.

Off to the hospital we went once more. The cast was back on, and I spent another eight weeks attempting to be more cautious. However, that didn't quite work out.

Eventually, the cast was removed, and for a while, I managed to avoid further incidents. Then one day, I was invited to play at a friend's house. Oh, the excitement of new adventures! We were playing outside, and they had a marvelous tool shed. At least, that's how I perceived it at that age. My friend dared me to jump off the tool shed.

You probably don't need to second-guess my response—I said yes. This time, the height was even greater than before. I never once considered the consequences after experiencing such events throughout the year. *Third time's the charm,* I thought.

I climbed up the tool shed effortlessly, as going up was never the problem. It was the coming down that proved challenging. I focused intently, and upon hearing their signal to jump, I propelled myself off the shed with all my might! And yes, you guessed it, I broke my arm once again.

Off to the hospital for the third time. This occasion required surgery due to the extensive damage. And, as you might have predicted, it was the same arm and the same place. After three incidents, my parents were investigated for child abuse. I spent nearly a year in and out of casts, all because of my unwavering belief that I could fly. While it was true in one sense, it was never going to work out in the physical realm.

Beliefs can be beautiful, except when we fail to question whether they truly serve us. We can often get hurt because we are unwilling to let go of a belief, repeating the same patterns and thoughts, convinced that there is no other way.

As we move forward, let's cultivate curiosity about the beliefs that no longer serve us. Be open with yourself, for you are the only one who needs to address this at present. You are the one who will feel the effects of a belief that no longer serves you.

Beliefs

What exactly is a belief? According to Webster's dictionary, a belief is "to consider to be true or honest, to accept the word or evidence of." Take a moment to reflect on a belief you hold. As we tune into that belief, it feels true to us. It provides a sense of safety and security, creating a framework that makes our external world feel more predictable.

But what happens when someone questions our belief or holds an opposing thought? Is it easy for us to let go of our belief? Do we cling to it even harder or feel compelled to prove that we are right?

We witness this dynamic frequently in politics and religion. It used to be a commonly advised rule to avoid discussing politics or religion because these topics can shake the very foundation of where a person stands. They often lead to immediate conflicts rather than uniting us.

So, what occurs when beliefs are passed down from generation to generation? Over time, we may stop questioning why we hold these beliefs to be true. Instead, we unconsciously internalize the idea that changing these beliefs would be disastrous. Perhaps we are even told that we *must* hold these beliefs, or else something terrible will happen.

This is particularly evident in the realms of religion and politics. If things do not go a certain way, we might be told that we will go to hell or that the world will be destroyed due to a wrong decision. Let's revisit the definition of *belief*. Could it be that a belief is based on a set of conditioning that leads us to a particular set of thoughts and information, supporting that belief and creating an illusion of safety?

A belief is formed within our mental energetic body, operating like a computer program until we consciously decide to upgrade it with a different program. If we never take the time to examine the programs running within us, they will continue to function as they were initially set.

It is crucial to be aware of what we believe and determine if these beliefs truly align with our intentions and values.

Now, let me share a story about how our beliefs shape our perspectives. This story is from Yogananda: "My faith and belief are better than yours." It's like blind men arguing about the descriptions of an elephant they have been washing.

"One blind man had been washing the trunk, so he claimed the elephant was like a snake. Another blind man, who washed the leg, insisted that the elephant was like a pillar. Yet another, washing the massive sides, described the elephant as a wall. The man cleaning the tusks confidently declared that the beast was nothing more than two pieces of bone. And the man handling the tail was convinced that the elephant was a rope leading up to the heavens! Finally, the driver said, 'Friends, you are all right, and you are all wrong.' Each blind man had only experienced a part of the elephant, so they were partly right, but also wrong because they lacked the complete picture."

Our beliefs often contain elements of truth, but there are often aspects that we miss. This is known as relative truth.

Epigenetics and Generational Patterns

Now, let's journey back several generations in your family lineage. What circumstances were unfolding? Was there slavery, famine, war, or abuse? What kinds of beliefs do you think your family formed to survive? Were there hidden family secrets or undisclosed children born out of wedlock?

Each of us carries something from our ancestral lineage, and sometimes we aren't even aware that these deep-rooted programs or conditioning are operating beneath the surface. They become automatic responses, and when they are challenged, our reactions may seem extreme to others, as if our very lives were under threat.

It's important to understand that when something remains unprocessed or unaddressed, it becomes stored within our physical and energetic bodies. When a couple conceives a child, that child inherits an imprint of everything that occurred several generations prior. Just contemplate the power of someone deciding to do this inner work—to commit to changing patterns from the past, present, and future. Allow that notion to soak in for a moment.

According to The National Library of Medicine website, research in the field of epigenetics has shown that traumatic events from generations past can still manifest in subsequent generations. For example, studies have revealed a higher prevalence of PTSD in Holocaust offspring who have experienced their own traumatic events, which have been associated with maternal PTSD in the Holocaust survivors themselves (Yehuda and Lehrner, 2018).

In an article on transgenerational trauma and the role of epigenetics, it is explained that epigenetics explores cellular variations caused by external environmental factors that "switch" genes on and off, resulting in changes in the phenotype of genetic expression without altering the DNA sequence or genotype. Epigenetic effects have been observed in the offspring of traumatized parents, and there is evidence that some of these effects can be observed in third-generation offspring as well (Krippner and Barrett, *Journal of Mind and Behavior*, Winter 2019, Vol. 40, Issue 1, p53-62, 10p).

What is intriguing about this research is that if we were to compare the astrological chart of grandparents with that of their grandchildren, they often exhibit close similarities. In many cases, we are more similar to our grandparents than to our parents. So, what happens when our grandparents experienced trauma, and their grandchildren display similar symptoms despite never personally experiencing those events?

The efficacy of memory recovery through hypnotherapy has always been a subject of debate. When examining the research, we see that sometimes we may not be processing our own trauma, but it still affects us as if we had experienced it firsthand. This could come from generational trauma or conditioning from our families or society, whether from our family stories or family traumas. What matters most is not the retrieval of specific memories but rather the positive changes that occur within the person, both internally and externally.

To further complicate matters, we must consider a person's past lives and the unresolved issues they may still carry from those lifetimes. When a lifetime comes to an end, we leave behind the physical body, but our soul continues, taking every experience with it. Energy cannot be created or destroyed; it simply changes form. Not all of those experiences are conscious in our current life. This can be discovered in hypnotherapy or other modalities that work in this area.

In fact, most of those memories do not need to resurface because that particular lifetime has concluded. However, sometimes we experience glimpses or echoes from past lives, and these can influence our present life. There are even television shows featuring young children who vividly remember their past lives and can provide verifiable proof of events that they could not have known about otherwise.

Occasionally, we may find ourselves drawn to certain periods in history, which can indicate that we carry cellular memories from that time and may have unresolved matters to address. Personally, I am not a proponent of exploring past lives solely for the sake of entertainment. I believe it is a complete waste of time and energy. The focus should be on the present lifetime and the work that needs to be done here and now.

If something from another time and place is holding you back, that is a different matter. In such cases, it becomes necessary to go back and heal whatever is causing conflict for the individual. I've had numerous clients ask me, "Were all my past lifetimes terrible?" Of course not. The purpose of this current life is to examine the faulty thoughts we hold *about* those past lives and how they have created a reactive self connected to these flawed beliefs. Once we discover and correct this, we will no longer be bothered by these things.

However, it's important not to misunderstand. Sometimes, we may need to recognize the positive aspects of who we are, but more often than not, this desire stems from the ego's curiosity about potential fame. When past life regression is approached with the intention of healing, it goes beyond being a mere entertaining journey and becomes a powerful, transformative experience. As infinite beings, we have created many experiences to explore our creative abilities. It would be unreasonable to think we could accomplish everything in just one lifetime. It's not a matter of "one and done" when we exist as infinite beings.

According to Yogananda, the concept of reincarnation was removed from literature to encourage individuals to make changes in their current lives instead of waiting for the next lifetime, being trapped in an endless cycle of reincarnation. Unfortunately, people did not fully utilize the opportunities presented in their current lifetimes to release and heal what was necessary to break free from the wheel of karma. Therefore, it didn't serve the purpose they had hoped for.

As you can see, we are not always aware of these underlying factors. For example, a family line may struggle with anxiety, depression, or substance abuse. Could it be that these responses stem from something they no longer need to carry?

In my own experience, my husband used to tease me because I would shop as if I were feeding twenty people. I didn't know how to cook smaller portions, which led me to spend excessively on food. When I would look into my kitchen cabinets, a strong sense of anxiety would arise, as if we might starve if they were empty. This fear consumed me, and the only remedy was to ensure we had enough food stocked up. This belief didn't originate from my personal experiences but was deeply ingrained within me. If my husband questioned this belief, I would become upset. My body and mind would remain on edge until that fear was appeased, which meant having enough food in the pantry. The fascinating thing about beliefs is that once we change the information we consider to be true (such as the belief that we may starve to death in the next two weeks unless we have more food), which is often rooted in fear, we can experience a more positive response. Merely being willing to explore where these beliefs come from and how they may serve us (particularly our ego) opens up the possibility of profound transformation, not just for ourselves but for our families as well.

Since our brains have an automatic survival response, these beliefs can run deep. We may come up with countless reasons to justify why we should cling to these beliefs. This became even more prevalent during the pandemic. When faced with chaotic and unpredictable situations, both individually and collectively, we held onto these beliefs even tighter. We felt an increased need for them because our survival felt threatened, right?

It becomes challenging to surrender and let go of these beliefs without having something else to hold onto. If only everyone would do things the way we believe they should, then the world would be a better, calmer place! Yet, we can observe the opposite is true.

When our fears take over and we try to persuade others to alleviate our fears by conforming to what makes us feel comfortable and safe, it becomes a losing battle. The reason is that we are not engaging the executive functioning portion of our brain. Instead, we are operating from the reptilian brain, which is solely focused on survival. It presents us with two options: do what is necessary to survive or face death.

Naturally, we choose what we believe will ensure our survival, disregarding the rest. We're alive, so cheers to another day! However, the next day is trapped within that same belief system, preventing us from having any experiences other than the ones we "believe" we should have. Our opportunity for growth and expansion comes to a halt.

Anyone who has experienced anxiety knows that it can greatly restrict our world. Anxiety takes control and dictates the limitations of our environment. We feel the need to confine ourselves within this narrow framework, fearing that anxiety might overpower us. Paradoxically, this belief only exacerbates the anxiety because when an anxiety attack occurs, it feels as if we are on the brink of death. We then try to exert even more control over our environment to prevent this from happening again.

We may start avoiding certain places or even have to cease working to maintain this sense of control. If you or someone you know has gone through this, they can attest to the difficulty of breaking free from this belief. The only way to work through and release anxiety is to open up our environment and begin creating positive resources to deal with it if it arises. Relying solely on external factors to make anxiety disappear will ultimately lead to failure.

So, how do we recognize the beliefs that are causing suffering for ourselves and others?

First, we must identify these beliefs. What falsehood or lie are we holding onto? While this belief may seem true to us, we must evaluate how it manifests in our lives. Does it bring us peace, or does it trigger fight, flight, or freeze responses? When someone challenges our belief, does it ignite anger and an unwavering commitment to defend our position?

If we have a strong response, it is likely a fear-based reaction that can be transformed into an expanded and loving response. When we lean into that space and truly listen to what it is telling us, it generates the energy of willingness to let go of the baggage holding us back and step into our true creative potential.

Often, ego-driven beliefs permeate various aspects of our lives and create disharmony. These beliefs may be considered relative truths, as they shape our perception of the world based on learned experiences from childhood. For instance, a child who witnessed their parents navigating the victim triangle—comprising the roles of victim, persecutor, and rescuer—may internalize the belief that love equates to codependency and manipulation.

Consider this example. The father yells at the mother, blaming her for everything that is wrong (persecutor). The mother cries, feeling undeserving of such treatment (victim). The child, in an attempt to protect the mother, becomes the rescuer. As a result, the father feels isolated and alone, while the mother and child form an alliance against him (with the father becoming the victim and the mother and child the persecutors).

This cycle continues, with roles shifting among the family members. The crux of the issue lies in the belief that love is synonymous with manipulation to gain control. The truth, however, is that no one truly has control because they all play the role of persecutor. Once this realization dawns, individuals can take ownership of their lives and initiate change. Stepping out of the victim triangle requires assuming 100 percent responsibility for personal reactions and behaviors. This is the space where transformation becomes possible, as we work to change our thoughts, behaviors, and beliefs.

The second step is to observe our feelings in relation to these beliefs. We may experience fear, anxiety, anger, sadness, or shame. Recognizing and acknowledging these emotions indicate that we are moving in the right direction. In the example provided, the individual might feel a sense of loneliness and disconnection, likely accompanied by a combination of anger and sadness. Their underlying desire is to find an authentic connection, which contrasts with their current belief system.

The third step is to locate the emotions and beliefs in our body. They may be held in different areas, so take the time to explore and connect with your body. Close your eyes and turn inward, setting the intention to uncover where these patterns reside. Notice any feelings, sensations, or intuitive knowings that arise. Each time an event occurs and remains unprocessed, the body retains it until we address it. Recall the concept of COEX discussed earlier, where layers of trauma accumulate. During traumatic experiences, we often hold our breath as a survival mechanism. However, remember that conscious breathing supports processing, releasing, and healing. Eventually, we need to return and release these stored beliefs to prevent reliving them repeatedly.

The fourth step, if possible, is to connect with the specific part of your body where the belief resides. If you can touch it, place your hand on that area. By establishing this connection, your intention will guide the body's response and provide the necessary information to release the block. Visualize this part of your body having its own color, sensation, and shape. Recognize the body as a remarkable vehicle and respond to where trauma is held within it. Ask yourself questions like: What happened in my life to create this belief? How did it make me feel? How did it alter my sense of self? Did I lose a part of myself during that event? What gift or talent did that part hold? Remember to keep breathing consciously, using a consistent breath moving in and out. The body can finally let go of the belief, allowing for an upgraded and more positive response in your life. This step often initiates healing by attentively listening to what your body wants to reveal.

The fifth step is to continue breathing into your body. The breath activates the stagnant energy and belief. Ask this part of your body what needs to happen for the release to occur. Take your time with this step. You may receive messages in the form of feelings, images, thoughts, or sensations. Pay attention to all of them, as they each hold significance. It's possible that the message might indicate the release won't happen until certain conditions are met. If that's the case, make note of the changes that are necessary and the steps required to make them happen. Sometimes, taking the first step is enough to set the movement in motion, with further steps being revealed along the way.

The last step is the most exciting one. Now, consider your new belief. Notice the fear that was previously present has dissipated. By identifying the root cause, you can release the pattern and make wiser decisions for yourself. This belief has transitioned from the unconscious to the conscious mind, shifting to the prefrontal cortex where new decisions can be made. You'll observe that with a deeper understanding of how this belief truly impacted your life and what had to be sacrificed to hold onto it, formulating a more positive and loving belief becomes easier. In the given example, the individual may realize that love is not about control, victimhood, rescuing, or persecuting. Love is about openness, honesty, and caring, expressing feelings in a way that honors the truth of oneself and others.

After clearing out the stuck belief, it's important to continue focusing on your new belief or affirmation. An affirmation serves as a powerful tool to reinforce that this new belief is your truth now.

On a side note, if the experience you're addressing is highly traumatic, it's crucial to seek the assistance of a professional to process it, especially if it becomes too triggering to handle on your own.

As we can see, this process shifts a relative truth into an absolute truth. The relative truth is based on our belief system, and we might use it to validate our perspective. However, there is always another side to relationships, one that involves respect and taking ownership of our contributions. For instance, someone may believe that friends in happy relationships are either dishonest or that they themselves don't deserve such happiness. This is a prime example of a relative truth. By holding onto this belief, they will inevitably attract relationships that align with their negative view, leading to their eventual downfall.

In the next chapter, we will delve deeper into how these beliefs, stemming from faulty thoughts, impact us on a physical, emotional, and energetic level. This process not only facilitates the transformation of generational patterns but also aids in releasing stagnant patterns within our bodies. These patterns can manifest as disease and other underlying issues that may go unnoticed by individuals.

Divine Feminine

A gentle embrace that says I have been with you forever. You are my Divine Child. Peacefully I breathe into this space. I have always been loved. I will always be loved. A timeless space where she lies waiting for me as always. Peacefully her embrace lets me know, let it all go. Allowing the compassion and grace to fill my soul, releasing the pain, I am the creator of my world. I can now see what she means. Sincerely my heart opens like a rose opening to the sun. I am now open to receive your wise gaze. You have given birth to me and understand who I am. No conditions. I can now go into the world with your touch of love and compassion and create a world anew, a place connected to my love. Let it grow. Let it grow. I have always been loved. I will always be loved.

As a young child, I was unaware of the lack of positive role models for women. The few representations of women I saw on TV tended to be sexualized and portrayed as serving the needs of men. I remember watching shows like *Wonder Woman* and *Charlie's Angels* and admiring their strength and power, but also realizing the unrealistic nature of their portrayals, such as fighting crime in high-heeled boots and wearing provocative outfits.

I must have been around four or five years old when these shows aired (my math skills aren't the best, so the timeline might be a bit off). A year or so later, I came across a t-shirt that said, "Anything that boys can do, girls can do better!" It instantly became my favorite shirt, not because of its appearance but because of its message.

The shirt conveyed that I, as a girl, was just as important and capable as boys. It affirmed that I could do anything boys could do, and perhaps even do it better. I was not meant to serve them; I was their equal.

For many women in the '70s, this was their everyday reality. They didn't know any different because nothing different was shown to them. Looking back, it's hard to believe that during those times, if a woman became pregnant, she would eventually become unable to find employment. The career choices available were typically limited to becoming a nurse, secretary, or teacher, and this perspective was widely supported by both men and women.

As the '80s came along, women had to take on more roles due to rising divorce rates. They could no longer solely stay at home with the children; they had to earn a living and often raise their children on their own.

If you were to watch shows from that era, you would see women wearing large shoulder pads, symbolizing their ability to do what men could do. However, the downside was that women were *shouldering* the burden of both worlds. They became exhausted and realized that what they thought they wanted wasn't as great as it seemed.

This led me to wonder:

- ❖ What does it mean to be a woman in a world dominated by male energy?
- ❖ What is the significance behind this?

After attending a class where someone asked about feminine energy, I found myself uncertain of how to answer that question. The teacher didn't provide a clear answer either, leaving me in a state of contemplation.

Living in a world of duality, we tend to think that being female means we cannot embody the masculine, and vice versa. While there is currently much discussion around this topic, I want to take this chapter in a different direction.

What I want to emphasize is that both masculine and feminine energies exist within all of us. If we are female, we energetically embody the masculine as well. Similarly, if we are male, we energetically embody the feminine. Take a moment to let that sink in.

Now, what does this realization mean for us?

We have both masculine and feminine energetic fields within our system. However, for the most part, the world has been predominantly influenced by masculine energy until recent years. As women started advocating for greater equality, they often employed masculine energy to assert themselves. We have taken the masculine energy as far as it can go, and now we are witnessing a resurgence of the feminine energy in the world. This shift is occurring because we have reached the limits of what intellect alone can achieve. If we were to continue solely relying on intellect, we would become severely imbalanced, potentially jeopardizing our survival.

It is crucial to recognize that we need both masculine and feminine energies to maintain balance. These energies complement each other and contribute to a more harmonious existence. Our perception of masculine and feminine energy is often shaped by what we observed from our parents during our upbringing. In the past, there were wise teachers, medicine men or women, and shamans who guided us in understanding and integrating these energies. However, in our current culture, we must actively seek this knowledge as it is not readily available. Many of us are only aware of what we were shown as children.

If we were to search for books or resources on the topic, we would likely find an abundance of male gurus and spiritual teachers, with fewer representations of the feminine ones. Women were not considered authorities when regarding God or spirit though there are certainly many important female figures in a variety of religions.

However, I predict that this disparity will gradually balance out in the future.

Here's an intriguing observation: the energy of our planet is feminine. Mother Earth is a highly evolved living being that embraces and supports every one of us. She reflects back to us the consequences of our creations, whether through weather patterns, global warming, or societal issues. Everything in physical form embodies feminine energy. For example, when we are seeing all of the wildfires, what are they telling us about our anger? The flooding is an expression of our over emotional ways. When we start to become aware that she is reflecting our collective energy, it is a powerful example of what we are creating.

We are progressing toward aligning more with the Divine Mother, who provides an abundance of space and opportunities for us to remember our true nature. The feminine energy is characterized by sensitivity, intuition, love, and the power of creation within us. It manifests as unconditional love and emanates a peaceful aura. In Chinese medicine, it is often represented as the black or yin energy. Although I personally dislike the association of black with negativity, it symbolizes the potential and power held within the feminine energy.

When the feminine energy is balanced within our bodies, it facilitates a positive flow of creation, which is then carried out into the world by the masculine energy. During our formative years, we often look to our mother figures as the representation of feminine energy. If we perceive our mothers as weak, manipulative, angry, disconnected, overly sexual, or unreachable, we may develop a distrust for this energy within ourselves. While in the womb, we are unable to differentiate between our own energy and our mother's. Thus, whatever experiences or emotions our mothers go through during pregnancy, we absorb and establish patterns within our own system. Although this is not a conscious process, these patterns influence our external and internal worlds, shaping our perceptions without our conscious understanding of their origins.

Once we begin to explore and understand these patterns, it can bring profound healing to a person's life.

On the other side of the spectrum, we have the masculine energy, which is considered the positive pole of the feminine energy. It represents the yang aspect and embodies mental energy. This energy propels us outward into the world and also serves to protect what the feminine energy creates.

In our society, the masculine energy has often been portrayed as the stronger of the two energies. However, many societal portrayals demonstrate the lower functioning of the masculine energy. Men are conditioned to believe that showing emotions is a sign of weakness. They are encouraged to take what they want without consideration, as if it is their entitlement. This portrayal is often seen in leadership positions both of companies and nations. Society conditions us to believe this is the epitome of proper masculinity. As a result, men may suppress their pain and emotions, leading to dissatisfaction, high blood pressure or other physical conditions, and a sense of discontent with life.

Consider your own perception of what it means to be male. Reflect on your father's characteristics and how you perceive your own masculine energy functioning in the world. Although the father does not physically carry the baby, the sperm carries its own energy, which influences the child. This operates on a cellular level, even if we are not consciously aware of it due to the absence of language.

For men who have been taught to conform to society's expectations of masculinity, integrating a balance between their masculine and feminine aspects can be a struggle. Similarly, women who adhere to society's beliefs about femininity may also face challenges in finding a balance between their masculine and feminine sides.

There should be a flow within the body between the masculine and feminine energies. The feminine energy brings about creation, nurturing, and a sense of direction, while the masculine energy helps manifest these creations in the external world. The mental energy of the masculine side paves the way for the feminine energy's expression. There is a supportive and protective balance between these energies, with the masculine serving to protect the feminine so she can freely create.

Another perspective to consider is how our intimate relationships can mirror patterns from our childhood. For example, if one's mother was emotionally intense and unpredictable, they might unconsciously seek a partner who is emotionally detached. Alternatively, they may attract someone who is also emotionally unpredictable and unstable. This provides opportunities to heal their relationship with their mother. However, what initially seemed like a good fit can become an issue in the relationship, as the partner may not express emotions or may be emotionally unavailable, leading to instability in the person's life. This demonstrates the lower functioning of the ego with respect to the integration of the masculine and feminine sides.

However, through healing work, individuals can recognize that their feminine side has been suppressed, preventing them from fully experiencing and expressing emotions. This suppression has burdened the masculine energy, forcing it to overcompensate. By exploring their thoughts and beliefs surrounding this dynamic, integration and upgrading of the masculine and feminine energies can occur.

As individuals engage in deeper work with the masculine and feminine energies, they may develop a more androgynous appearance. A great example of this can be seen in Yogananda, who embodies the balanced integration of these energies.

This is an opportune time to embrace and understand both aspects of our being and how they function in our lives. Our True Self is responsible for love and working in harmony with the Divine Mother.

By honoring the feminine aspect of the divine, our hearts expand with love. This expansion breaks down barriers that may have been erected due to trauma and rejection, dispelling feelings of unworthiness and a sense of not being wanted.

With this expanded understanding, we are able to hold space for others, fostering unity as we recognize that both masculine and feminine energies flow within each of us.

I once had a teacher who explained that when a child exhibits neurodivergent behavior, it can be a reflection of the parent's lack of integration with their own emotional aspect. (Neurodivergent is an individual that differs in their neurological functioning like autism.) The parent may have predominantly relied on their mental faculties for processing, neglecting the role of emotions. It's important to note that this is not solely determined by genetics but also learned behaviors that have been passed down through generations. By healing and integrating within ourselves as parents, we can positively influence our children. This healing has far-reaching effects that extend to future generations.

We are currently experiencing a phase of energetic shifts that seek to restore balance from where we have been. This balance is essential for us to evolve into a better way of relating to one another. Rather than attempting to change the external world, our focus should be on transforming our inner world—bringing our mental and emotional bodies into harmony. This internal alignment allows for physical healing and the release of what no longer serves us, propelling us toward higher levels of spiritual connection.

Our Energetic System

What once was this body will become so much more! This body has served in this earthly existence, but it is not who I am. I am not just this body. I am the wave and light of spirit that flows into the ethers, each thought creating my reality, and each pulse shifting my reality. I am not this earthly body; I am so much more. Each wave of love flows out into the universe, shifting my reality. I am not just this physical body. I am the manifester of my world and light. Each thought is shifting what I share with the world. I am connected to all the elements of the Earth. Be aware of how they are balanced inside of me which shifts my reality outside of me. I am not just this earthly body.

Within our Western way of thinking, there is great emphasis on the power of science and measurable phenomena. However, history has shown that when we are on the cusp of something new and expansive, it is often met with criticism, and we question its relevance. If something cannot be measured or seen, it is deemed nonexistent. Nevertheless, in recent years, science has begun to validate what has been known for thousands of years. Researchers such as Lynne McTaggart, Bruce Lipton, and others have demonstrated the existence of an energetic field that surrounds our bodies. Ayurvedic and Chinese medicines have recognized this for over 5,000 years.

Growing up in a family with several medical professionals, these concepts were rarely discussed or acknowledged. If we fell ill, we simply visited a doctor who prescribed medication to alleviate the symptoms. However, my perspective started to shift when my sister was diagnosed with cancer.

Unbeknownst to us, the neighborhood we lived in had been exposed to contaminated water resulting from improper disposal of chemicals by a dry cleaner and hospitals. Similar to the situation in California, where Erin Brockovich discovered contamination, we experienced high rates of mutated cancers in our area. Many women also experienced unexplained miscarriages. Although we moved away before the issue was identified, the damage had already been done to my sister, Kathy.

Kathy was diagnosed with an advanced and aggressive form of cancer while she was pregnant. I couldn't help but question why she was the only one affected, despite the whole family residing in the same house. Logically, if the chemicals were so toxic, we should have all been affected. But that wasn't the case.

After a challenging battle, Kathy succumbed to cancer and passed away, leaving me at the age of twenty-seven and her young son who was a year and a half. I questioned my own fate—would I also die young? It was during this time that the universe presented me with an unexpected opportunity: to take a Reiki class. At the time, Reiki was not as well-known as it is now. This was my introduction to energy medicine—an enchanting realm that had always existed, unbeknownst to me.

This newfound knowledge shed light on the questions I had about how we create our reality. Since that moment, my journey of exploration and learning has continued. I delved deeper into Ayurvedic medicine, which approaches the human body in a holistic manner. The combination of energy medicine and Ayurveda helped me grasp the profound connection between our thoughts and the manifestation of our reality. It became clear that tending to our physical bodies with care and wellness is essential, but so is nurturing our thoughts, as they shape our entire existence.

It is crucial to note that this perspective is never intended to assign blame to individuals for their illnesses. Such thinking does not yield anything beneficial. Instead, it offers an alternative viewpoint, a different path to navigate through our reality. Remember, we are here to evolve and expand, and sometimes catalysts arise to aid us in this process. My hope is that by sharing this, it will help you find a clearer and faster path to your own growth.

So, let us embark on a journey, traveling back in time. Let us imagine that we have chosen to incarnate on this Earth to learn and share our unique gifts with the world. In this process, we do not possess physical form as we do here on Earth, as it is unnecessary.

As our soul energy descends, it is accompanied by the ethereal energy. Ether is the energy that creates the space within us. It is the essence that encompasses spirit or source. It represents the realm of infinite possibilities. This energy flows down our spinal cord, permeating every aspect of our being. It provides the space needed for our joints and all the intricate spaces within our bodies.

The element of ether corresponds with the thyroid and parathyroid glands. Ether is contained within the sushumna, the energetic channel that houses the ida (negative or feminine energy) and pingala (positive or masculine energy). Visualize this energy flowing down the center of your spine with the ida and pingala oscillating based on their electrical charge, always returning to the sushumna at the core. This process gives rise to the chakra system within our bodies. From the element of ether, the element of air emerges.

Air represents our mental energy. It is the realm where our thoughts take shape, initiating the process of creation. It holds tremendous power, as it can elevate us to a higher vibration of creation or pull us down to a lower vibration. The air element is associated with our lungs, heart, skin, ankles, and kidneys. It encompasses the thymus gland, located very near the heart. When the air element is balanced, we can create in a beautiful and harmonious manner. However, an excessive air element may manifest as symptoms resembling ADD, leading to an imbalance within the system and difficulties in following through with tasks, as thoughts tend to race. Conversely, a contracted air element may result in obsessive tendencies and an inability to let go.

When someone is described as "airy," it immediately conjures an image of an individual with an excessive air element. Such individuals may even appear disconnected from the grounding of the Earth as they walk. In astrology, the signs Gemini (mutable), Libra (cardinal), and Aquarius (fixed) are associated with the air element. The air element corresponds to the heart chakra.

Moving on, we encounter the element of fire. Fire ignites passion and provides direction to our thoughts. It is the spark that focuses and propels us in creating with zeal. The fire element resides within our muscles, eyes, head, stomach, and thighs. It encompasses the pancreas. For instance, consider how fire transforms. The same heat is necessary for our bodies to break down food into the nutrients needed to support the various systems and tissues of the body. But when out of balance, we may experience digestive issues leading to diarrhea, and feel depleted. Also, individuals with a fiery nature often possess a staccato voice.

Those who struggle to embrace their personal power tend to hold the energy of the fire element in their thighs, representing the negative pole of the fire element. Conversely, individuals harboring intense anger may manifest it through their eyes. The liver is the organ associated with the anger, and those with excessive anger may develop liver issues. Additionally, individuals who consume alcohol frequently tend to exhibit bursts of anger. Thus, it is advisable to approach liver detoxification cautiously, as excessive release of toxins can trigger the processing of anger. The fire element is connected to the solar plexus chakra. In astrology, the signs Sagittarius (mutable), Aries (cardinal), and Leo (fixed) are associated with the fire element.

Moving further, we encounter the element of water. Having passed through the fire, which provides direction, the water element nurtures and imparts the necessary creativity and emotions to our thoughts. As we delve into the water element, the vibration becomes denser. The water element resides in the lymphatic system, regenerative organs, bladder, and circulatory system. It corresponds to the ovaries and testicles. If an unhealthy creation persists without a shift in thought process, it may manifest as chronic physical conditions, including potentially cancerous conditions. However, a positive creation indicates that we are nearing the completion of a beautiful manifestation. The water element is associated with the spleen/sacral chakra. In astrology, the signs Pisces (mutable), Cancer (cardinal), and Scorpio (fixed) are associated with the water element.

Last, we encounter the earth element. I often perceive the earth element as the one responsible for organizing intricate details. However, it can also cause us to become fixated on the wrong aspects, hindering our ability to move forward. Imagine an individual so entrenched in their ways that no amount of persuasion can elicit a change. They become inflexible, incapable of embracing anything different. I envision our internal system becoming rigid, resembling dry soil that cracks and rejects what may be beneficial. The earth element resides in our bones, large intestines, teeth, and legs. It encompasses the adrenal glands. In astrology, the signs Virgo (mutable), Capricorn (cardinal), and Taurus (fixed) are associated with the earth element.

Just like the creation and our entry into this world, our system is now complete, ready to embark on our life purpose. These elements compose our bodies, connecting us to Mother Earth. She lends us this body to have our human experience. When we fulfill our purpose, our bodies return to where they belong—with Mother Earth. The body serves as the vehicle for our life journey. When traumatic events occur within the system, the energy can become stagnant, stuck, or overexpanded, resulting in dis-ease. As the system progresses, the elements begin to descend, creating our complex and interconnected system. The sushumna, a neutral energetic channel running down the center of our being, serves as the main portal from which the pingala and ida energy channels branch out.

The pingala represents the positive and masculine pole, while the ida represents the negative and feminine pole. However, it is important to note that these terms of *masculine* and *feminine* are not limited to societal definitions. In this context, the ida represents the space of creation, embodying intuition, creativity, and compassion. The feminine energy is associated with yin, as when we initiate a new creation, it connects with all possibilities, similar to how if a child mixes all paint colors together, black is the composite color. On the other hand, the masculine energy is the mental aspect that takes the energy of creation and brings it into the world. It is directive, intelligent, and acts as a healthy protector of the feminine energy when used appropriately. The ida is located on the left side of the body and connects with the right hemisphere of the brain, while the pingala is on the right side of the body and is connected to the left hemisphere of the brain. In terms of the nervous system, the parasympathetic nervous system (PNS) is connected to the feminine side of the body, while the SNS is connected to the masculine side.

When we observe the sushumna with ida and pingala, we can see that it forms the caduceus, which is also the symbol used in the medical field to represent healing. If the symbol is overlayed on the body, we see that it features two intertwined snakes (ida and pingala) that ascend to the third eye located in the middle of the forehead. It symbolizes the electrical pattern of the negative (feminine) and positive (masculine) poles. These poles create a push-and-pull relationship, continually drawing toward each other. The wings of the caduceus represent the two hemispheres of the brain, while the upright staff (in alignment with the spine) signifies the path of finer energies, leading to the central part of the brain depicted by the rings and the spinal cord below. This symbol represents the Tree of Life in ancient traditions. The two serpents symbolize the dual aspect of the Mind Principle. The fiery breath of the sun represents the positive pole and vital energy on the right side of the body, known as *yang* in Chinese tradition and *pingala* in Hindu tradition. The elevated masculine side holds wisdom. The cooling energy of the moon essence of nature flows on the right side of the body, referred to as *yin* in Chinese tradition and the ida current in India. The feminine side holds love. The caduceus, which connects us to the inner Tree of Life, allows us to work from the center outward. The yin energy regulates the currents of thoughts and feelings, bringing us back to the center and spirit. This is often considered the middle path or way in some traditions.

The pingala holds the energy of thought (wisdom), while the ida holds the energy of feeling (love). Intelligence without love remains mere intelligence. Wisdom cannot be attained without love. This is developed through years of spiritual practice yielding a higher awareness that there needs to be a balance with these two energies containing the masculine (logic) and feminine (love) which allows wisdom to emerge. The energetic connection between the pingala and ida brings the energy back into the sushumna, the central energy channel.

The caduceus symbolizes the kundalini energy held within the body. The kundalini energy is the movement of spiritual energy without disruption up the spine to connect with higher spiritual realms to awaken this inside of you. In ancient times, the pharaohs wore this symbol on their crowns, signifying their understanding that when this energy rises to the third eye, it triggers a spiritual awakening through the kundalini experience. However, it is crucial not to approach this process haphazardly. When the kundalini energy awakens, everything held within the body, both positive and negative, is released. If an individual has not done the necessary personal work, they may have to confront all their emotions, traumas, etc., simultaneously. Premature activation of the kundalini energy can result in severe disruptions to the individual's electrical system.

Originally, the term *chakra* referred to the chariot wheels of the invading Aryans, symbolizing the sun. People of that era, who could perceive the energetic body, described it as spinning wheels of light. In the traditional system, there are seven main chakras. However, in Human Design, the system has expanded to include a nine-chakra system after a split in two different centers.

The root chakra, located at the base of the spine near the perineum, is associated with the earth element and the color red. It pertains to survival instincts and our physical form. The root chakra holds fear, and it grounds us to the Earth upon our entry into this world.

When our energetic field expands from our physical body, the area closest to the body where it can be felt is often the densest. For example, individuals with lower back issues are often dealing with fears related to their connectedness and safety on Earth. This can include concerns about finances and whether they will have what they need. Energetically, this densest element in the body is comparable to the earth element, which, like the Earth itself, does not move rapidly. Developmentally, this element corresponds to the stage of conception to six months old, which is the bonding stage. Spiritually, this energy holds the energy of completion or the death process, as well as themes of separation and fear of death/separation.

Moving up the energetic system, we come to the sacral chakra, located in the lower belly just below the navel. This chakra relates to the water element and is associated with the color orange. It is the center of feminine energy, emotions, and conditional love. The sacral chakra is responsible for vitality, creativity, and sexuality, and it houses our inner child. Developmentally, this chakra corresponds to the stage from six months to eighteen months old, which involves learning to trust the universe and starting the journey of releasing control, shame, and victimhood.

The solar plexus, located beneath the rib cage, corresponds to the fire element and is associated with the color yellow. It represents our personal power and holds our mental energy and masculine energy. Often, we may use our mental energy to try to control our emotions, which can disrupt our creative and healing processes. The mental energy is connected to the young adult phase, where individuals may have learned to view feelings as problematic and attempt to suppress them. This developmental stage spans from eighteen months to three years old.

Issues that arise in the lower chakras can affect the upper chakras, as everything is interconnected within the body. For instance, when a young child is told to suppress their emotions, they may learn to hide their them and control their feelings. This can lead to a disconnection from their True Selves and affect their expression in the world (throat chakra). Similarly, if a young adult is taught to prioritize hard work and suppress emotions, they may overexert their solar plexus (achiever), causing the sacral chakra to shut down. This, in turn, can impact their perception of others with judgment (third eye) and their ability to express themselves (throat chakra). These are simplified examples of how dysfunction can manifest in the system, but it's important to remember that each individual's experience may differ, creating a unique chess game of energetic dynamics.

The heart chakra serves as the bridge between the lower chakras (root, sacral, and solar plexus) and the upper chakras (throat, third eye, and crown). It is located over the sternum and represents the air element. The heart chakra is the space of unconditional love or Christ Consciousness, embodying care and compassion. Its color is green. It corresponds to the developmental stage of socialization, which spans from three to seven years old. This stage involves cultivating unconditional love, forgiveness, and a spiritual connection based on love and worthiness rather than fear.

The heart chakra allows us to expand beyond the limitations of ego and connect with our higher selves. It is symbolically represented by the intersection of the two parts of the cross in Christian practice, the four directions in shamanic tradition, and the point just before the branches form in the Tree of Life.

Moving up to the throat chakra, located in the throat itself, we encounter the element of ether, associated with the color blue. This chakra is the divine expressor. Issues related to expression often stem from blockages in the sacral chakra, where emotional suppression occurs. When we are unable to fully feel and express ourselves, the throat chakra may become blocked. It is connected to the thyroid and parathyroid glands and serves as the space within us that allows spirit to manifest and create beautiful things. When the throat chakra is blocked, individuals may experience issues such as strep throat, neck problems, or hormonal imbalances related to the thyroid. It relates to daily spiritual practice and the ability to express devotion and love, as opposed to inhibition based on fear and shame.

The next chakra is the third eye, also known as the divine eye. It is located in the middle of the forehead, between the eyes, and its color is indigo. The third eye is associated with vision and intuition, but it can also house the inner judge. When we judge others, we immediately disconnect from our spiritual connection with Spirit/God. The third eye represents mental love. Developmentally, it corresponds to the stage of adolescence, spanning from twelve to eighteen years old. During this stage, the focus is on connecting with guides, teachers, and angels, as opposed to living in illusion and feeling isolated from God.

The last chakra is the crown chakra, situated at the top of the head, and its color is violet. It is where we hold the energy of our life purpose and can connect to our pure divine essence and angelic self. Developmentally, this chakra corresponds to adulthood. It is the stage where we accept God as the ultimate authority, letting go of grandiosity and authority issues. However, the crown chakra can become closed off if we fear allowing connection to flow in.

The Universal Laws

As we have explored our energetic system, we may have noticed patterns in how we were created. Within our internal system, we have access to the laws of the universe. These laws are housed in our chakra system and gaining control and understanding of them leads to becoming a master in coherence. But what does that mean exactly?

The chakras are containers of different dimensions within our bodies. When the Bible speaks of holding the spirit of God inside us, it holds truth. Although there are seven laws of reality, they can be understood as seven subsets of the same law. Each chakra carries a different energy related to the first law, which is mentalism.

The Law of Mentalism

> *"The Universe is Mental – held in the Mind of THE ALL."*
> —The Kybalion

Mentalism is the universal law that states everything is created from a thought. This law states mentalism is contained in the crown chakra. Everything we consciously and unconsciously experience is the result of a thought form that manifests into reality. If something shows up in our lives, it is our creation, no one else's. If we are not conscious of it, then it is being created in the unconscious part of our reality. When we think something, it creates a vibration that is sent out and returns to us in a corresponding form. This doesn't mean that if something negative happens to us, we created it, but how we perceive and work with it is what we create. There will always be ups and downs and disruptions in life, but how we focus our thoughts through these experiences is key.

The Law of Correspondence

> *"As above, so below; As below, so above."*
> —The Kybalion

The law of correspondence states that what we create within ourselves, we see outside of ourselves, and vice versa. This law is related to the third eye chakra. In relationships, we often see in others what we have yet to acknowledge within ourselves, whether it is our shadow or golden shadow. This is because we are following the law of correspondence. It helps us see, like a mirror, what the outside world is reflecting back to us about what is happening within. Every thought is connected to a vibration, and the goal is to create harmony and agreement in our manifestations.

The Law of Vibration

> *"Nothing rests; everything moves; everything vibrates."*
> —The Kybalion

The law of vibration states that every thought creates a vibration. It is fitting that this law is connected to the throat chakra. Every thought and spoken word carry a vibration that interacts with the law of correspondence, reflecting back to us. Our words hold great power, and what we think, whether spoken or not, will come back to us. Even unspoken thoughts carry a vibration, so we should not deceive ourselves into thinking they don't matter just because no one else can hear them. They do matter.

The Law of Rhythm

> *"Everything flows out and in; everything has its tides; all things rise and fall; the pendulum swing manifests in everything; the measure of the swing to the right is the measure to the left; rhythm compensates."*
> —The Kybalion

The law of rhythm teaches us that everything flows and has its own timing. This rhythm can be high or low and is associated with the heart chakra. Each thought carries a vibration and rhythm, connected to time. When the vibration is low, time seems to move slowly, and when it is high, time appears to pass quickly. Sometimes, to reach higher levels, we need to go low first. The concept of "we can only go as high as we are willing to go low" comes to mind. Rhythm and vibration are closely connected. The vibration determines the rhythm of movement. If we don't like what we are manifesting with our thoughts, things will slow down. This provides an opportunity to experience the lows and find ways to grow and expand.

The Law of Cause and Effect

> *"Every Cause has its Effect; every Effect has its Cause; everything happens according to Law; Chance is but a name for Law not recognized; there are many planes of Causation; but nothing escapes Law."*
> —The Kybalion

Vibration and rhythm come back to us as an effect, as stated in the law of cause and effect. Every cause has an effect, and vice versa. This law is associated with the solar plexus chakra and can also be seen as the law of responsibility. We are responsible for what we create through our thoughts. Our thoughts generate vibrations, which can be high or low, and these vibrations create rhythm. This rhythm, in turn, leads to cause and effect. If we send out messages of love from the heart, love will quickly return to us. If we spend our time creating negative thoughts and judgments, we will attract others who do the same. We are the ones responsible for these creations. By understanding our own vibrations without judgment, we can identify their source and make necessary shifts, thereby altering the vibration, rhythm, and the corresponding law.

The Law of Polarity

> *"Everything is dual; everything has poles; everything has its pair of opposites. Like and unlike are the same; opposites are identical in nature but different in degree; extremes meet; all truths are but half-truths; all paradoxes may be reconciled."*
> —The Kybalion

The law of polarity is also connected to the law of creation, which corresponds to the sacral chakra. Everything has a negative and positive pole, and every creation has a magnetic pole that pulls in one direction or the other. This magnetic pole is related to our DNA. When we consider epigenetics and the laws of creation, we can understand how our creative process affects us on a physiological level and influences our DNA. This process aids in our evolution. The lower we can go, the more power we have to rise up. We discern the distinction between warmth and coldness, for example, and in music, the difference between middle C compared to lower C or higher C. What we may label as absolutes, such as good or bad, are actually part of a scale in a particular direction.

Instead of ignoring our shadow side, we can embrace and upgrade it, allowing us to connect with the true essence of who we are.

The Law of Gender

> *"Gender is in everything; everything has its Masculine and Feminine Principle; Gender manifests on all planes."*
> —The Kybalion

Everything is created through the interplay of the masculine and feminine principles. These principles are present in every aspect of life, and we cannot have one without the other. This law is associated with the root chakra. The feminine aspect exists internally, while the masculine aspect carries that feminine creation out into the world. As mentioned earlier, the caduceus symbolizes the magnetic poles of these principles, and there is a balance between the negative and positive in creation.

Each of these laws helps us understand how to navigate the different dimensions and realities we create within and outside of ourselves. When we truly embody these principles, we can achieve and understand the power of who we are and how we manifest in the world. It is through our thoughts that we create our reality, and by delving into our unconscious beliefs and thoughts, we can more rapidly shift our vibrations and rhythm.

While each chakra holds different energies, we can recognize their interconnectedness and how they work together. Understanding the energetic flow within our system empowers us to mindfully change our world. It encourages us to challenge faulty thoughts and beliefs that hinder us from creating the reality we desire. We possess free will to choose the plane of reality in which we wish to exist.

Our Wise Soul Within

We are many, we are one. The little one asks, "What does that mean?" You are much greater than you think you are. You have a special spark of light that you brought to this Earth from God to share with the world. Each spark of light connects you with everyone else's light to make the whole. But your light holds a certain gift that no one else can share. You are so much more than you think. But you must remember to find this inside of you. It has always been right there inside of you, the True Essence of who you are.

Wise Soul/True Self

Have you ever wondered what all this talk about your True Self is? Aren't we simply this physical body, capable of thinking, speaking, hearing, smelling, tasting, and seeing? Shouldn't we be aware that our True Self is also a part of us? The part of us that has not forgotten our connection to God and all of our live experiences.

I often encounter clients who express that they have no idea what their True Self is. I would have said the same thing twenty-something years ago. However, there is a significant distinction between the ego and the True Self.

I recall a time when my youngest son was determined to save a squirrel. This was one of his many attempts to rescue wild animals, including birds, turtles, opossums, chipmunks, geese, raccoons, mice, and even flying squirrels. During the COVID pandemic, we had an influx of animals needing assistance. For him, helping an animal in need was a way to regain control in a world that felt completely chaotic.

At that time, we already knew the squirrel was sick. He insisted that the only way the squirrel would survive was if he took it in. We had learned from past experiences that this was not the case, despite his genuine intentions to help. He was adamant about keeping the squirrel for just one night.

The next morning, as he prepared to go to school, he claimed that the squirrel was safe. We searched for him but couldn't find the squirrel. I had a feeling he had it somewhere nearby, but he refused to disclose its location. Little did we know, he had hidden the squirrel on his shoulder under a jacket.

Off to school he went, accompanied by the squirrel. This poor creature was abruptly taken from its natural environment and taken to a place filled with children and noise. News quickly spread throughout the school that there was a squirrel inside the building.

The school administration intervened, informing my son that he could not bring a wild animal into the building for valid reasons such as disease transmission and disruption to the learning environment. We were called, and both my son and the squirrel were taken home. He firmly believed that the squirrel's demise was due to being placed in a box, disregarding the fact that the squirrel was already sick and the stress of being removed from its habitat exacerbated its condition.

No matter what anyone said, he refused to accept it. He was devastated by the school's actions. To him, the squirrel was like all the other animals he had encountered. If the animal didn't survive, it felt as though he himself wouldn't survive.

I would have loved to explain to him that his ego was in control, driven by fear that life was uncontrollable and that something terrible could happen at any moment. This was his attempt to exert control, only to realize he had none. However, when fear dominates our thoughts, we become closed off and resistant to feedback and introspection.

When our ego experiences pain and hurt, it becomes difficult to reach someone. Occasionally, though, we connect with our True Self, which possesses profound wisdom. Even in the most challenging times, we can experience a sense of peace, knowing that everything is being taken care of. It is crucial to recognize the differences between our ego and our True Self. They are vastly distinct.

Our True Self exists in a state of non-duality. It recognizes that things are not simply black or white. The notion of "I am right, you are wrong" does not exist within this realm. It embraces expanded ideas and possibilities, embodies humility, intuition, love, and a deep connection with nature. It encourages honesty, understanding that the self is an illusion, and possesses wisdom and harmony. It does not form opinions, but rather perceives the higher self's connection to Source/God as the ultimate truth. It believes in unity and has a keen awareness of illusions that the ego often fails to see. It is the wise part of ourselves that comprehends what is best for us. Within the True Self, we think in a "both/and" way, instead of "either/or," and we recognize that if we are right, it doesn't necessarily mean the other is wrong.

When the ego has not undergone its healing work, it tends to be arrogant, angry, rude, harsh, stuck in the past, resistant to authority, unhappy to be alive, unwilling to listen, unforgiving, selfish, emotionally charged, full of self-doubt, prone to dissociation, avoiding healing, and exhibiting tendencies toward addiction. The ego makes it impossible to see how many people can be right at the same time. It confines us into the either/or thinking and forces us into believing we should be against those who don't side with us or believe what we believe.

Every individual possesses the capacity for a wise part, often referred to as the higher self. The higher self guides individuals in making wise and healthy decisions. The Wise Adult or True Self represents the higher consciousness that understands our purpose and acknowledges the divine spark within us. It recognizes our connection with everyone else, allowing for diverse options in our lives.

When we make decisions based on a foundation of love, we tap into a larger perspective of what is possible, and we identify the solutions required to navigate challenging situations. It becomes evident when someone is operating from this space, as it is devoid of selfishness, anger, degradation, or any other lower vibrational energies. They would not justify their actions by claiming they are acting in their own best interest while leaving a trail of destruction in their wake.

This is the shadow side of the ego masquerading as the higher self, when in reality, it is a wounded part that only seeks its own desires without considering the impact on others. However, it is important to remember that what we send out into the world is reflected back to us, allowing us to see how our behaviors and beliefs affect our lives and the lives of others.

There may be options that initially shock individuals, but in the end, they serve the highest good of everyone involved. Often, when working with individuals, we reach a point where we transition to a higher dimension of living, rooted in compassion and love. Love and compassion are not about dwelling in self-pity and recounting the hardships of life, but rather about shifting into a space where we take responsibility for our own patterns. With compassion and understanding, we acknowledge that we were doing the best we could until we knew better, and now that we know better, we are willing to make a change.

If I sit through session after session listening to clients' victim stories, I would not only be doing a disservice to that person, but I would also be perpetuating the problem by allowing the energetic pattern of such behavior to become further ingrained in their energetic field and body. This shift can be initially jarring to the system, as the pattern is rooted in suffering and pain. When there is attachment to a story, even if it doesn't serve us, challenging that story often leads the individual to defend and reinforce it.

As we delve deeper and expand our perspective, it becomes the most loving and compassionate act to transform these patterns into something infused with light. The more we let go of what we are not, the more we will realize the greatness of what we truly are. Engaging in deep inner work through hypnotherapy or other therapies strengthens our connection to our wise self. We become more attuned to this aspect of ourselves, and from there, waves of positive change ripple out into the world, impacting more than we might expect.

Our lower mind or ego tends to have limited ideas about what is possible in life. The lower mind/ego resides in the lower three chakras of the body: root, sacral, and solar plexus. On the other hand, the higher mind, located in the upper chakras (heart, throat, third eye, and crown), elevates us to higher vibrational frequencies of healing and potential. It is essential to remember that the heart serves as the bridge connecting the lower and upper minds. While issues may manifest in any chakra, they generally originate in the lower chakras.

To recap, negative thoughts and beliefs affect our physical and energetic bodies, including the emotional, mental, and spiritual aspects. This doesn't mean that they won't manifest in the upper chakras, but their origin lies in the lower chakras. For example, if a young child was taught that being creative is problematic, this belief would take root in the sacral chakra and subsequently impact the expression of the sacral chakra. The throat chakra is connected to the sacral, therefore, the throat chakra has issues with having a true expression of who they are due to the shutting down of the creative energy. This would affect our authentic expression and how we would express ourselves. As we heal these areas, the corresponding symptoms will also dissipate from wherever they had manifested.

Let me share with you a story about the journey of our souls in this world. Imagine, for a moment, that God is a beautiful source of unconditional energy or light. This divine light permeates everything, desiring expression in limitless ways. Within this limitless space, God's energy starts to manifest as the most exquisite flower ever created.

This flower boasts magnificent petals, each with its unique gifts and frequencies. Each petal harbors its own community, much like our families. Upon closer inspection, we realize that even within each petal, there are countless variations. Every petal represents a soul family, seemingly similar yet distinctly different upon closer examination.

As the petals move further away from each other, the differences become more pronounced. However, just like the flower, all the petals remain interconnected. Each petal is connected to God, and within that connection, they carry the light of God. In the words of Jesus from John 14:12, "you can do all that I can do and much more."

This story serves as a reminder that we carry God's light within us and have the capacity to achieve all that we desire (and even more) if we remember this truth. When a soul decides to embark on its journey into this world, it plans to depart from its soul family, much like a child leaving home for college. The soul plans what it wants to learn and grow in this human experience. It could involve continuing from a past life, completing unfinished business, or exploring something entirely new. This journey is a tremendous gift, and pre-planning before birth is a fascinating concept (as exemplified by my three-year-old at the time, who claimed to have meticulously selected his perfect parents and couldn't wait to come into this world, though he would vehemently deny it now at fifteen years old).

So, this soul petal ventures away from home and arrives on Earth. However, like most adventurous souls, it chooses a path where other parts of its soul family are not present. After all, what could it learn from being surrounded by such similar energy? That's not to say that it won't encounter some soul family members along the way, but experiencing the same thing repeatedly would be like living in a perpetual Groundhog Day. We need some variety to spice things up. And so, the soul petals embark on their individual journeys.

During this process, the most exquisite fabric is woven from the different energies as they arrive on Earth, each soul learning and growing from one another. If we imagine ourselves as unique pieces of this fabric, connected to the whole but unable to see it due to our individual vantage points, we might perceive ourselves as being alone. However, this perception is deceptive because we are always connected to so much more.

But here's the catch: in order to grow and gain understanding, souls *need* to forget who they truly are. They must forget that they originate from the divine spark of God and that they are meant to share their light with the world. As a soul petal begins its journey to Earth and crosses the veil into this earthly plane, its memories of God and connectedness start to fade.

If the soul were to remember its true nature, it would not truly experience the depths of learning. This amnesia takes hold, particularly as we start to engage with the external world, which typically occurs around the age of four or five. However, if we listen to young children, they often possess great wisdom and memories of certain things. But as the soul petal embarks on its journey, it embraces the desire to extract the utmost from this experience, which requires encountering obstacles to gauge its progress. Along the way, these sparks or even explosive moments serve as reminders of who they truly are.

As these intersections of life occur, there is an opportunity for redirection and remembrance. In fact, simply intending to understand who we are and why we are here sets us on a journey. Yet, like most journeys, we are tested, not as a form of punishment, but as a means of polishing away what no longer serves us. It is our responsibility to lean into this process and recognize that it shapes us into the beautiful diamonds and pearls we are meant to be.

Now, embarking on a spiritual journey comes with a disclaimer: it will test us. We have a choice to lean into it, explore where it takes us, and release what no longer serves us. Alternatively, we may resist expansion, growth, healing, and letting go, allowing the ego to dominate and operate from lower levels of functioning. A spiritual path is not synonymous with religion; it is about supporting our unique journey. Each path leads to the same destination. However, once we grasp certain concepts and step out of ignorance, we can no longer claim we don't know.

At this stage, we begin to learn that this work is truly about releasing what was never truly us, enabling us to step solidly into who we are meant to be. This process does not erase our personality; rather, it refines and sheds the layers that have obscured our vision of ourselves and others, allowing us to have a different experience. As our understanding of ourselves becomes clearer, our intuition, insights, and inner senses start to open and become stronger and more distinct. Here are some of the shifts we may notice:

Releasing allows for an increased capacity to tap into creativity that was previously hidden. Creativity is not limited to artistic endeavors but encompasses every thought we generate. If we spend most of our time creating stories based on faulty beliefs such as unworthiness or helplessness, there is little room left to create beautiful things like a delectable meal, a loving note, a painting, writing a book, creating a podcast, planning a garden, connecting with nature, or cultivating inner harmony. Releasing these energies frees up space for greater creativity and flow in our lives.

The root chakra is our connection to the world and our perception of ourselves. If we hold feelings of inadequacy, fears, and insecurities about our identity, we hinder our ability to be fully present in our earthly existence. Without a sense of worthiness and belonging, life can feel like an ongoing struggle. Stagnant energy becomes fixated on our own concerns, preventing us from fully engaging with the opportunities around us. The root chakra houses our life force energy, and if this energy is blocked or stagnant, it impedes energy flow in other areas. By recognizing and embracing our inherent brilliance and unique light, we shift the focus away from ourselves. Strengthening our presence in the world allows energy to ascend the sushumna, opening us to higher levels of awareness and liberation.

The sacral chakra is associated with our emotional body and how we feel about ourselves. When we harbor fear, resentment, guilt, and sadness, there is little space left for joy, enthusiasm, and creativity. It's akin to a passionate child whose intense emotions can quickly clear a room. Their demands are immediate and unwavering. When our emotions dominate us, they can create destruction in our lives. However, when they are balanced, they serve as guidance, showing us where we are in any given moment. By releasing and healing this energy, we tap into the passion and vitality needed to transform our inner world and achieve optimal healing. Sometimes, I wonder how empowering it would be if we were all aware of the wonderful cheerleader within us, constantly whispering, "You've got this, boy/girl! Keep moving forward because it only gets better and better as you release those darker energies." (I envision my cheerleading outfit being like the cheerleaders on *Saturday Night Live*.)

The solar plexus chakra is the seat of our healthy power and self-confidence. It's where we store our faulty thoughts and beliefs about power misuse. In some instances, individuals who seem heartless in their pursuit of success may have an immature solar plexus energy. They may develop a God complex and believe that everyone is beneath them. This energy can also manifest as the persecutor archetype. Healing this unhealthy achiever archetype leads to True Self-confidence and a sense of healthy power. It enables us to recognize when enough is enough and when we need to take a break, preventing burnout caused by incessant striving and doing.

The heart chakra is the center of unconditional love. When guarded, it forms a cold, impenetrable wall that obstructs caring and numbs our own feelings, as well as our capacity to care for others. Behind this wall, a fear of being unlovable persists. However, when we open this chakra, it creates a warm, radiant space of love and light. Remember, the heart is the bridge between the lower and upper chakras. With a healthy ego (solar plexus) and an open heart, we achieve a harmonious balance of healthy power, love, and humility. This state allows us to understand our true essence and engage with life in a more coherent and loving manner.

The throat chakra is our divine expressor, responsible for manifesting God's expression on Earth. However, if there are unresolved issues in the sacral chakra, such as a raging emotional state, the expression that emerges may not resemble the divine being of energy but rather a disruptive lightning bolt. The ability to express oneself comes with the responsibility to do so with a caring voice, sensitive to the impact our words may have on others. Those who have experienced emotional abuse are acutely aware of the damaging vibrations that words can carry. This form of abuse is often referred to as psychic murder, as the vibrations of hurtful words can tear away at a person's energetic field, leaving them weakened and vulnerable to illnesses and many never recover.

The third eye is associated with vision and mental love. It holds the creative will of God and serves as the seat of our inner judge. If we find ourselves judging ourselves or others, we shut down our visionary capabilities. This chakra may lay dormant until we begin to activate it. By addressing the inner judge and releasing its energy, we awaken this dormant area and invite spiritual vision into our lives. The third eye also plays a crucial role in balancing the right and left hemispheres of the brain. Positioned in the center of the brain, its activation can lead to the awakening of other untapped areas, such as the pineal gland. This activation brings forth enhanced abilities that were previously inaccessible, such as telepathy, clairsentience, claircognizance, clairvoyance, and clairaudience.

Telepathy refers to the ability to connect and communicate with others through thoughts, bypassing the need for spoken language. If we were aware that others could perceive our thoughts, our world would be vastly different. This heightened awareness would bring greater focus to the quality of our thoughts and their true impact. I once had a conversation with someone who proudly proclaimed that they only *thought* negative things about others, as if it were a virtuous act because they didn't speak it aloud. However, judging is judging whether it is internal or external. Engaging in gossip and negative thoughts for the sole purpose of spreading negativity generates harmful energy that lowers the vibrations of everyone involved. By silently observing and saying nothing, we are equally complicit in the negativity as active participants.

Clairsentience refers to the ability of empaths to pick up on the vibrations and emotions of others, as well as the energy of a room. While most people can sense when something is off in a room, empaths can deeply feel and sense these disturbances, often perceiving the truth behind spoken words. Personally, I've always been more attuned to the energy of situations rather than the words being said, which has allowed me to gain a deeper understanding of what is truly happening. This ability has also kept me safe in dangerous situations by guiding me toward the right actions to navigate through them.

Claircognizance is the ability to have clear knowing. It often manifests as a sudden understanding or knowledge about something, even when we don't know how we came to possess that knowledge. Personally, when claircognizance occurs, I feel a gentle settling within me, a sense of truth and understanding that my conscious mind might not have been aware of before.

Clairvoyance is the ability to have clear seeing, often associated with the third eye chakra. It can manifest as visual images or scenes in the mind's eye, or sometimes as seeing something with our physical eyes that others cannot perceive. My family often jokes that when they see me looking past them, they know I'm tapping into my clairvoyance. While most of the time it's a visual experience in my mind, I also have a sense that the energy I'm perceiving is right behind the person. It's important to note that these intuitive senses operate through the same channels as our imagination. Individuals who experience these senses may initially think they are making things up, but if they follow the guidance, they often find it to be accurate. I always encourage approaching these senses as a game at first because judgment (from self and others) can shut down the channel.

Clairaudience is the ability to have clear hearing. We may hear messages either audibly, as if someone is talking to us, or within our mind. It's important to distinguish that this is not schizophrenia, as it is not a delusion and doesn't negatively impact a person's functioning. These senses are not disorders; rather, they are higher forms of communication that allow us to connect with the spiritual realm. These abilities were always meant to be a part of who we are, but at some point in history, they were associated with the devil. It's similar to the character of the Church Lady from *Saturday Night Live*, always asking, "Could it be Satan?" It's important to discern that if the information we receive is loving and would never harm anyone, it is not coming from a negative source. If it carries the energy of the ego, it is simply the ego speaking. Spirit operates with love, compassion, wisdom, and neutrality. Additionally, many individuals who possessed these gifts in past lives, during times when they were not understood, were often persecuted or killed. This can lead to a deep fear in the current life of being discovered and facing similar consequences. However, as we do the inner work and heal, these fears dissipate, allowing us to embrace our gifts with freedom and find peace. I spent a significant portion of my life hiding my abilities out of fear. While there may always be individuals who attack out of fear, I choose to remain in the light and love, rather than remain hidden in a closet, denying the truth of who I am.

Last, the crown chakra is the center of our pure Divine Connection. It houses our angelic self and our kinship with all of life. It grants us a deeper understanding of our purpose in life, not based on what we do, but on who we are. If someone has disconnected from their connection with God, for any reason, it will be felt here. This disconnection affects our understanding of ourselves and can lead to a sense of loneliness in the world.

As we shift these old patterns and embrace our higher selves, we begin to experience life in a radically different way. It's like telling all our wounded inner children that we've arrived to change the course of their lives. They no longer have to pretend to have it all together because a wiser part of us has taken over, expanding their vision of who they are. This transformation alters their presence, how they perceive themselves, how they think about themselves, how they care for themselves and others, how they express themselves, how they see themselves, and how they understand their purpose.

As we embrace the release of what no longer serves us, our True Self begins to emerge more prominently in our lives. There is a greater sense of peace and calm, even in the face of twists and turns. We discover a path that connects us to our True Self, guiding us through difficulties. Our inner children no longer run our lives in ways that are detrimental, but instead, they learn and expand in more beneficial ways. We gain insight into how the shadow side operates and creates confusion and fear. Once we become aware of these patterns, they lose their power, and we gain the ability to make choices that align with our true desires. This shift in perception allows us to see the world from a panoramic view, offering us a multitude of options for unity and connection in a higher way of being.

Astrology: The Road Map to You

When I was younger, I was always curious to discover more about my purpose in life. I explored various avenues in search of clarity and guidance. I attended different churches, hoping to find answers, but often left without any greater sense of direction. Books that could provide insight were scarce at the time. However, as I've grown older, I've come to understand that we are the creators of our own reality. Everything that enters our world has a purpose. Astrology, as a science, can help illuminate why we are here, what karmic patterns we are working through, what wounds we are healing, and what lessons we have already become proficient in.

Astrology has been utilized for thousands of years and offers a profound understanding of the focus of our current life. The planets represent the macrocosm or the outer reflection of who we are. When planning our incarnation, we specifically choose the time of our birth to align with the purpose of this lifetime. This doesn't negate our free will, as we still have countless choices in life. However, having a representation of the position of the planets during the moment of our birth, also called our birth chart, allows us to navigate challenges with greater ease, providing us with tools tailored to our individual journey. It's like having a shortcut to assist us on our path, a roadmap that reminds us of our destination. Engaging with a skilled astrologer who can help us understand our chart and its intricacies enables us to use this guidance to enhance our lives. As we progress, some individuals may no longer require external guidance as they develop a strong connection to their own intuitive understanding.

Here are some basic elements of an astrological chart. The chart consists of twelve zodiac signs that guide us through the year. The first three "houses" in the astrological chart (labeled 1, 2, 3), form the psychological quadrant, include Aries, Taurus, and Gemini. The second quadrant is the sociological quadrant, comprising Cancer, Leo, and Virgo. The third quadrant is the philosophical quadrant, encompassing Libra, Scorpio, and Sagittarius. Last, the fourth quadrant is the spiritual quadrant, represented by Capricorn, Aquarius, and Pisces. By visually observing these divisions, we can gain an initial understanding of the themes we are working on in this lifetime based on the placement of planets.

The first house corresponds to Aries and Mars. It symbolizes how our thoughts drive us in the world and represents our physical body and personality.

The second house corresponds to Taurus and Venus. It relates to money, possessions, and the gifts we receive.

The third house corresponds to Gemini and Mercury. This house governs communication, whether through writing or speaking.

The fourth house corresponds to Cancer and the Moon. It represents our home and family.

The fifth house corresponds to Leo and the Sun. This house pertains to our social life, creativity, and love life. It reflects how we are perceived in the world.

The sixth house corresponds to Virgo and Mercury. It encompasses health, work, and minor illnesses.

The seventh house corresponds to Libra and Venus. It represents our close relationships, both in business and romance. This is also where matters such as lawsuits, agreements, and contracts are addressed.

The eighth house corresponds to Scorpio and Pluto. It relates to sex, death, and investments, including income, loans, and mortgages.

The ninth house corresponds to Sagittarius and Jupiter. It signifies higher learning, philosophy, religion, and long-distance travel.

The tenth house corresponds to Capricorn and Saturn. It represents our career, ambition, and status, as well as our relationships with authority figures and superiors.

The eleventh house corresponds to Aquarius and Uranus. This house represents the collective brotherhood and sisterhood. It relates to our friendships, involvement in organizations, and pursuit of goals.

The twelfth house corresponds to Pisces and Neptune. It pertains to our subconscious, psychic abilities, spirituality, self-renewal, and unknown challenges.

The Sun represents our life personality and what we are meant to bring to the world. The Earth supports our Sun in fulfilling its purpose. The Moon signifies our passions and strong emotions. The South Node indicates our past experiences and lessons. The North Node shows the direction we are striving to move toward. Mars represents masculine energy and the area of personal power. Venus represents the feminine energy and governs our relationships. Saturn is the teacher, indicating where we need to continue learning and expanding. Jupiter reveals the blessings we receive once we have learned from Saturn. Neptune signifies our spiritual purpose. Mercury shows how we communicate our message to the world. Uranus represents the areas in need of healing. Pluto represents the interplay between the ego and soul. Last, Chiron, the wounded healer, indicates something we are meant to share with the world and gain wisdom from, even if we feel we haven't fully accomplished it yet.

As mentioned earlier, astrology is a complex field of study that can be explored throughout our entire lifetime. However, this overview provides a starting point for interpreting our birth chart and gaining a deeper understanding of who we are and the purpose we came here to work on. You can go to Astro-charts.com to get a copy of your free birth chart.

Human Design

The next tool that I find fascinating is Human Design, which combines elements of Eastern and Western astrology, incorporating the Chinese I Ching, Kabbalah, Hindu chakra system, and quantum physics. Similar to astrology, Human Design utilizes the date, time, and location of our birth to generate a personalized chart. This chart serves as a map of our unique design, providing insights into how we function, where our conditioning lies, and how to align with our authentic selves. One place to access a chart is geneticmatrix.com, but it may be worth it to invest in a skilled and trained professional to help interpret it.

Many of us have been conditioned to be someone we're not, often leading to a lack of awareness about our True Selves. By using the Human Design template, we gain clarity on whether we are living in alignment with our inherent nature or if there are areas that need healing and realignment. While many people associate purpose with what we do, Human Design reminds us that it's more about who we are.

Through the Human Design chart, we can discover our potential and bring a greater sense of direction to our lives. Instead of blindly navigating our path, we can confidently embody our true nature, make decisions that align with our design, recognize conditioning patterns, and work on releasing them to embrace our authentic path.

It's important to note that I will only provide a basic overview of Human Design. One of the first aspects to understand in Human Design are the different types, which encompass five distinct personality types. The first name is the quantum language created by Karen Curry Parker, founder of Quantum Human Design™ and the second is the traditional terminology: Initiator or Manifestor, Alchemist or Generator, Time Bender or Manifesting Generator, Orchestrator or Projector, and Calibrator or Reflector.

Initiator or Manifestor

Initiators are quite rare, comprising only 9 percent of the population. The Initiator is a type that possesses their own unique creative flow. They can exhibit qualities such as being energetic, impulsive, mysterious, and powerful. However, they may also struggle with anger, self-absorption, a lack of teamwork, and a tendency to be secretive. Initiators are often resistant to being told what to do, as it can hinder their creative process. This type has at least one motor center connected to the Throat center and does not have the Sacral center defined.

Two crucial questions for Initiators to reflect upon: Am I fully expressing my power, or am I hiding it? Is anger preventing me from fully embodying my power? To maintain harmony in the energetic field, Initiators must inform others about their actions and intentions. They may experience anger when faced with disruptions to their creative flow. Past experiences of having their power taken away can instill fear and hinder their willingness to take action. The challenge for Initiators lies in reclaiming their power and overcoming feelings of isolation. Their quantum purpose is "to initiate people into the frequency of transformation and creativity through direct access to the Quantum Pulse" (Parker 2021, 7).

Alchemist or Generator

The Alchemist is an individual who has come to master their craft through diligent work. They possess sustainable energy, self-awareness, and an energetic presence. However, they may also experience frustration, a tendency to give up prematurely, and a feeling of being stuck. While they have a defined Sacral Center, they do not have a connection from a motor center to the Throat Center, which is what distinguishes them from Initiators and Time Benders.

The Alchemist should contemplate the following questions: Am I fully expressing my skillful accomplishment, or am I settling for less? Is frustration preventing me from realizing my true potential? Alchemists must wait for external stimuli and respond to their environment in order to manifest effectively in their lives. Approximately 36 percent of individuals in the world fall into the

Generator/Alchemist category. When things don't seem to be progressing with sufficient momentum, Alchemists may experience frustration and be inclined to quit prematurely. However, if they exercise patience and wait a bit longer, they often experience a surge of inspiration that propels them to the next level. Endurance and maintaining faith in the Source represent the primary challenges for the Alchemist. Their quantum purpose is "to physically manifest creativity and express through devotion" (Parker 2021,11).

Time Bender or Manifesting Generator

The Time Bender is a blend of the Initiator and Alchemist types. They possess a defined Sacral Center and a direct motor connection to the throat. Time Benders are known for their high energy levels, multitasking abilities, proficiency in finding shortcuts, self-awareness, and sustainable energy. However, they may also experience anger, frustration, a tendency to skip important steps, impatience, and a propensity for leaving tasks unfinished.

Similar to Generators, Time Benders should ask themselves the following questions: Am I fully expressing my mastery, or am I settling for less? Is frustration hindering me from fulfilling my true potential? Approximately 32 percent of individuals in the world fall into the Time Bender category. Time Benders can feel frustrated and angry when faced with creative disruptions and insufficient momentum. They may also experience a sense of isolation and disconnection from their source. The primary challenge for Time Benders is to surrender and let go. Their quantum purpose is "to physically manifest creativity and accelerate the quantum process and linear time" (Parker 2021, 11).

Orchestrator or Projector

The Orchestrator excels in managing and directing others. They possess insight, intuition, and a magnetic energetic presence that amplifies the energy of the community. However, Orchestrators may be perceived as lazy, susceptible to burnout, highly sensitive, lacking self-awareness, and prone to bitterness. They have an undefined Sacral Center and no defined connections from any motors to the throat. Their strategy for creating in their life is to wait for invitations, which they often dislike hearing. Orchestrators make up approximately 20 percent of the population.

They should reflect on the following questions: Do I value myself or devalue myself? Is bitterness masking my inherent value? When Orchestrators do not adhere to their strategy, they can become bitter in life. They face challenges related to self-worth and managing their energy. At times, they may feel abandoned by a higher power. Orchestrators play a crucial role in holding the new energetic field within this realm, even if their contributions may not be readily apparent. Their quantum purpose is "to hold the energy template of what's to come and clear the vibration of the collective consciousness" (Parker 2021, 18).

Calibrator or Reflector

The Calibrator is known for being passionate and unique and they have a desire for a trusted sounding board to talk things through in order to come to clarity. They advocate for peace and prosperity and serve as a reflection of the health of their community. However, Calibrators can be highly sensitive, prone to disappointment, in need of consistency, struggle with staying grounded, and may exhibit clingy behavior. When you look at their charts you'll notice there is a lot of openness. They do not have any defined centers or channels, only the gates are defined.

Calibrators should reflect on the following questions: Can I "be" or am I "merged"? Is disappointment preventing me from fully embracing my authentic self? Their strategy involves clarity in decision-making and waiting to move through an entire lunar cycle before making a decision. Calibrators are the rarest of types as they make up approximately 1 percent of the population. They may experience disappointment when they witness unfulfilled potential and have a need for more time. Their challenge lies in having the courage to detach from misaligned situations and maintaining faith. The quantum purpose of Calibrators is to "measure through reflection the human condition and human potential" (Parker 2021, 22).

The Six Profile Lines

There are twelve profiles in Human Design, each a combination of two lines of the I Ching hexagram. The first three lines of the hexagram, or lower trigram, are introspective and learn by going inward, often exhibiting more introverted tendencies. The last three lines, or upper trigram, are interpersonal and learn through relationships. The upper trigram represents a transpersonal nature.

Line One–The Resource or Investigator: The Resource seeks a strong knowledge base rooted in fear. They have a deep desire to gather extensive information on subjects and individuals they engage with, creating a deeper connection. The Investigator is introspective and should ask themselves, "Are you afraid of the unknown?" Their quantum purpose is "to establish an informational foundation for the security and safety of others" (Parker 2021, 3).

Line Two–The Responder or Hermit: The Responder possesses claircognizant abilities, often knowing things without being able to explain how. They require time for replenishment and solitude to integrate the knowledge they absorb. Once replenished, they can re-engage with the world. The Hermit's unique energy often captures attention effortlessly. Without proper rest, they risk burning out due to energy depletion. They may appear shy or coy, requiring encouragement to connect with others. The Hermit should reflect on the question, "Are you hiding from life?" Their quantum purpose is "to integrate knowledge, energy, and wisdom, and await others' readiness to call upon them" (Parker 2021, 6).

Line Three–The Explorer or Martyr: The Explorer learns through discovery and experimentation, finding the best solutions available. However, they may develop a fear of making mistakes as they explore various options. By becoming experts in their chosen fields, they process and integrate their knowledge. They also explore relationships, breaking bonds that aren't working, and questioning relationships until around the age of thirty. The quantum purpose of the Explorer is "to explore and experience possibilities and share their experiences to protect and serve others" (Parker 2021, 9).

Line Four–The Stabilizer or Opportunist: The Stabilizer seeks stability and wants everything to remain intact. They have a contagious energetic field and enjoy connecting with their community. They are resistant to change unless they have a replacement plan in place. They fear losing everything they have and tend to be fixed in their identity, which makes them sensitive to criticism. In relationships, they may stay longer if they don't have another relationship lined up. Being in a state of limbo is challenging for them as they thrive on having a solid foundation. The Stabilizers should ask themselves, "Am I afraid of losing everything I have?" Their quantum purpose is "to establish a foundation of community and connection and pave the way for sharing and spreading ideas" (Parker 2021, 12).

Line Five–The Visionary Leader or Heretic: The Visionary Leader universalizes their experiences and knowledge to impact the world. They have a karmic draw to others and often evoke a sense of familiarity. Like the Hermit, they have a projection field that draws people to them. They are compelling and persuasive, seen as a saint by those willing to face their own healing, and a demon by those who resist. It is crucial for them to be in an environment that values their True Self. They may struggle with feeling unseen. The Visionary Leader's purpose is to resolve and heal karma. They should ask themselves, "Am I afraid to reveal myself?" Their quantum purpose is "to serve as a 'karmic mirror' for others, supporting the healing process through reflection, teaching, and sharing the highest potential of humanity" (Parker 2021, 15).

Line Six–The Adept or Role Model: The Adept evolves in three different stages. In the first thirty years, they operate as an Explorer (Line Three), engaging in experimentation and often experiencing turbulence. Around the age of thirty, they transition into the second stage which focuses on healing, observing, integrating, and personal growth. They may become more aloof during this phase, making it challenging to access their energy and relationships may be affected by their aloofness, but they need to recognize that they are searching for inner self-love. At around fifty, they transition into the third and final stage and are called back into the world as role models for others to observe and learn from. This is a time of being and fulfilling a sense of purpose. The Adept should reflect on the question, "Am I afraid of not fulfilling my destiny?" Their quantum purpose is "to experience, integrate, and demonstrate the highest potential of consciousness on the planet, quietly showing others how to live it" (Parker 2021, 18).

The Nine Centers

There are nine centers in the Human Design chart; these are similar to the chakras discussed earlier. When a center is colored in, it is considered defined, meaning it represents consistent energy that we show to the world, similar to someone's personality. Open centers, on the other hand, are white and represent energy that is not consistent and therefore influenced by those around us. Open centers amplify the energy present in that center.

Head Center–The Head Center is where ideas and inspirations are generated. It revolves around possibility thinking. It is also one of the two pressure centers and can create pressure to figure things out, whether defined or undefined. When defined, this center is an inspirational force. The Head Center is connected to the quantum field, which we can access through asking questions. Some questions to consider with the Head Center: Do I feel pressured to have all the answers? Do I trust the Universe to reveal the answers? Am I afraid of the unknown? Whose question am I trying to answer? In Quantum Human Design it is known as the Quantum Interface and the quantum purpose of this center is "to use inspiration and possibility thinking to trigger imagination and creative energy frequency" (Parker 2021). The core needs of the Head Center are decisiveness and self-trust.

Ajna Center–The Ajna Center is where information is stored and managed. When this center is open, individuals can see many sides to everything and are open-minded and fair. They do not have a fixed way of thinking. When defined, it is used to store information and the individual tends to see the world in a more black-and-white manner. Those with defined Ajna Centers do well with traditional teaching methods. It is an area of soul growth potential. Questions to ask from the Ajna Center include: Am I struggling for certainty? Am I afraid of uncertainty? Are my beliefs serving my highest good? In Quantum Human Design it is known as the Divine Translator and the quantum purpose of this center is "to translate inspiration into potential third-dimensional applications and imagine possibilities to stimulate creative energy frequency" (Parker 202). The core needs of the Ajna Center are decisiveness and self-trust.

Throat Center–The Throat Center is associated with communication and manifestation. It is essential for vitality. When the Throat Center is defined, it is designed for expressing through speech. Manifestors and Manifesting Generators have a motor center connected to the Throat Center and will therefore generally be and feel more heard. Generators and Projectors can have both open and defined Throat Centers but will not have a motor center connected to the throat, this is called non-motorized. Reflectors never have a defined throat. When the Throat Center is non-motorized or open, the individual may feel pressure to talk and may blurt things out to relieve the pressure. When someone with a non-motorized or open Throat Center is invited to speak, their words and wisdom is well received. Questions to ask for the Throat Center: Am I afraid of being invisible? Am I struggling for recognition? In Quantum Human Design it is known as the Activation center and the quantum purpose of this center is "to use language in an empowering, loving, creative way to stimulate and initiate sustainable, abundance possibilities" (Parker 2021). The core needs of the Throat Center are authenticity and vitality.

G Center–The G Center is associated with love, direction, and identity. It represents being at the right place at the right time and is the source of our Law of Attraction. If the G Center is defined, we tend to have a good sense of who we are. When it is defined, the question to ask: Can I be loved for who I am? When the center is open, the individual understands others' direction and amplifies the energy of someone with a defined G Center. It indicates intuition. If it is open, the question to ask is Am I lovable? In Quantum Human Design it is known as the Calibration center and the quantum purpose of this center is "to give direction to love, sustainability, leadership, empowerment, spirit, embodiment, natural order, compassion, and peace. It holds the magnetic resonance field of the magnetic monopole" (Parker 2021). The core needs of the G Center are lovability, decisiveness, courage, and authenticity.

Will Center–The Will Center is where we manifest on the material plane, particularly regarding money. It represents our value and self-worth. Money issues often stem from underlying self-worth issues. When the Will Center is defined, it is important to rest when needed and not rely solely on willpower for sustenance. When open, there may be a tendency to undervalue one's worth, which can affect the functioning of the monopole. Questions to ask about this center: Am I trying to prove myself? Am I trying to prove my value? In Quantum Human Design it is known as the Resource center and the quantum purpose of this center is "to align us with sustainability, community, truth, and value." The core needs of the Will Center are vitality, self-worth, and empowerment.

Spleen Center–The Spleen Center is the oldest center in the system and relates to survival, instinct, the immune system, and timing. It holds a gut-level pulse of fear and provides a knowing of the action necessary for safety. It is an awareness center rather than a source of power. When defined, individuals are designed to live in the moment and make decisions in the moment. They also have powerful immune systems. When open, access to constant "feel good" energy is not available. This can lead to challenges in letting go of addictions, whether related to substances or relationships. Individuals with open Spleen Centers tend to have more sensitive immune systems and benefit from natural medicine. There is unlimited intuition when the Spleen Center is open. A question to ask about this center: Am I holding on for longer than I should? In Quantum Human Design it is known as the Self-Actualization center and the quantum purpose of this center is "to give us the intuitive impulses about right timing for survival, health and wellness and economic action." The core needs of the Spleen center are self-trust and courage.

Emotional Solar Plexus Center–The Emotional Solar Plexus (sometimes referred to as ESP) is the center where we hold the most creative energy in the chart. It is where we experience emotions and use them to create the life we desire. When emotionally defined, decisions are made based on the feeling of what seems right, and individuals need time to make decisions. A consistent feeling of "yes" indicates a positive response, while a mix of "yes" and "no" indicates a "no" response. Challenges associated with the Emotional Solar Plexus include struggles for clarity, reactivity, and disappointment. When open, individuals may try to avoid conflict with emotions or try to fix them, both as ways to relieve the pressure from this energy. Questions to ask about this center: Is your baseline frequency abundant? Are you afraid to deal with truth and consequences? Are you trying to please everyone? In Quantum Human Design it is known as the Creative center and the quantum purpose of this center is "to hold the frequency of energy for abundance and faith." The core needs of the Emotional Solar Plexus are courage, emotional wisdom, empowerment, and decisiveness.

Sacral Center–The Sacral Center is the center of life force energy and relates to work in the world and sexuality. It provides sustainable energy for Manifesting Generators and Generators to do the work they are meant to do. While they may have sustainable energy, it is not meant for them to be work slaves. When the Sacral Center is open, individuals do not have sustainable energy and need to replenish and rest when signs of exhaustion arise to prevent burnout. Sometimes, they may realize they have gone too far before replenishing their energy. Questions to ask about this center: Do I know when enough is enough? Do I have the energy to sustain my choices? In Quantum Human Design it is known as the Evolution center and the quantum purpose of this center is "to respond with action to the needs of others, supporting the evolution of community and the expression of abundance and compassion" (Parker 2021). The core needs of the Sacral Center are decisiveness, courage, vitality, and empowerment.

Root Center–The Root Center is a pressure center and associated with correct timing. It provides a pulse to indicate when timing is right. The Root Center holds adrenaline energy and should be monitored to prevent depletion by acting before the correct timing. When defined, individuals receive the pulse for correct timing. When open, they may feel pressure to make things happen even when the timing is not right. Questions to ask about this center: What am I trying to get done to feel "free"? Do I trust in the timing of the Universe? In Quantum Human Design it is known as the Divine Timing center and the quantum purpose of the Root Center is "to receive and respond to what the Earth needs and wants as part of the evolution of the planet." The core need of the Root Center is vitality.

The Invisible Garment

Another great book I love to use is *The Invisible Garment* by Connie Kaplan. Connie Kaplan channeled this book after the death of her father. Angels asked her to write down thirty spiritual principles that help us understand the energetic fabric or purpose of our lives. While each of us has a unique fabric, there are several important factors to understanding our gifts and what we have come to learn in this lifetime.

The Sun represents our purpose for this lifetime, something we have decided upon before incarnating to learn more about. It is the sole focus of our purpose. The Moon represents an aspect of ourselves that we have become especially skilled at, so deeply woven into our fabric that we may not even be aware of its presence. Last, the Midheaven in our chart represents the energy that accompanies us throughout every lifetime. Those with the same Midheaven are part of our soul family. Often, we separate from our soul family because being around individuals who are too similar to us might hinder our growth.

Combining these two tools provides a comprehensive understanding of who we are. The following are the thirty principles Connie Kaplan wrote about, which give us a sense that what we carry in our fabric is different from what we might expect. It's important to note that our interpretation of these principles may differ from the typical definitions:

0: Placement,
1: Innocence,
2: Purity,
3: Memory,
4: Beauty,
5: Extension
6: Regeneration,
7: Generosity,
8: Goodness,
9: Awareness,
10: Reciprocity,
11: Flowering,
12: Creativity,
13: Intelligence,
14: Ecstasy,
15: Resistance,
16: Unity,
17: Attraction,
18: Focus,
19: Service,
20: Gratitude,
21: Harmony,
22: Dreaming,
23: Randomness,
24: Humility,
25: Desire,
26: Silence,
27: Peace,
28: Love,
29: Movement.

As we embrace our uniqueness and the gifts that only we can bring to the world, it becomes easier to let go of what no longer serves us. If you haven't explored Human Design or read *The Invisible Garment: 30 Spiritual Practices that Weave the Fabric of Human Life,* I recommend doing so to understand our individuality and that of our loved ones. As we enter the next chapter of our lives, we will explore ways to release conditioning that hinders us from being our True Selves.

Finding our Golden Shadow: Our Light Within

Oh, what a glorious surprise to find this way. It is a path connecting with the True Essence of who I am. The lifetimes I have wandered and searched, and it was always inside of me. This is the space I want to be in. It is a clearing of the middle way that brings me back to the True light of who I am.

Finding the Golden Shadow or Middle Path

This morning, as I sit down to write, I am reflecting on how often I have made things more difficult than they needed to be in life. I've observed my own behaviors and realized that certain shifts in my thought process could significantly improve my reality. However, in my younger years, it seemed almost impossible for me to make those shifts. How can we do something when we have no concept of it?

Over the years of working with clients, I have been fortunate to witness transformative experiences when individuals embrace higher expressions of themselves. By recognizing when our ego is in control and understanding the kind of life it creates, we gain the option to make a shift. Comparing this to the higher self that emanates from the heart and free from judgment, reveals the potential for a vastly different life experience.

As discussed in earlier chapters, our physiological system is wired to survive in challenging circumstances. Understanding why it behaves the way it does allows us to use appropriate tools to change the process. When we apply these tools to our lives and are willing to shift unconscious behaviors, conditioning, and thoughts, we can create an entirely new reality.

This process also enables us to connect more deeply with our golden shadow, the part of us that holds our higher truth, gifts, and unique self. We all have the capacity to shift our reality because we are powerful creators. Every thought we have contributes to the creation of our reality. By letting go of thoughts that no longer serve us, we generate a more positive outlook than ever before. This alchemical process transforms the very molecules that define us, changing the functioning of our brains and allowing access to higher levels of consciousness. Consequently, we become more resilient when facing adversity, leading to improved overall well-being.

Until now, we have explored the reasons why making these shifts can be challenging. However, we have now shifted our focus to how the process becomes easier and more magical as healing occurs. Remembering who we truly are makes it easier to let go of what we are not.

At times, resistance may arise when letting go of old patterns. It can feel addictive to hold onto pain and our stories, providing a false sense of identity. Yet, just like any addiction, it does not serve us as we might believe. Our system may perceive that experiences lacking extreme highs and lows are boring and not real. Sometimes, dysfunction and dissatisfaction must reach a tipping point before we are willing to embrace a better way of living. It is astonishing how individuals will cling to their suffering as if it were a badge of honor, which inhibits personal growth. This cyclic repetition keeps us trapped in the karmic cycle.

If I were to state at the beginning of this book that we are children of God and possess the spark of the divine within us, it might have seemed overwhelming. However, as we peel back layers of conditioning, we can gradually embrace this truth in a gentle manner. We are all connected to the same greatness, love, and light. By taking the time and summoning the courage to peel away these layers, we can authentically embody who we are, leading to extraordinary experiences in life as we align with our True Selves.

Take a moment to imagine how life has been when we carry unconscious behaviors from our family of origin, false beliefs, and past traumas. Each layer erodes our true essence, clouding our vision of the truth.

The truth is that we are divine beings who came to this world to offer our brilliant essence. In this lifetime, we have a remarkable training ground that allows us to see how our thoughts and feelings create our reality. It's important to remember that on the energetic plane of Earth, manifestation takes much longer compared to the spirit realm, where thoughts immediately become reality. Therefore, regardless of where we are on this journey, we are perfectly aligned with where we need to be. Each experience presents an opportunity to explore and heal, allowing us to discern if we are creating what we truly desire.

By investing time in this process, we accrue dividends not only in this life but also in everything that follows. There is no moment of failure; there is only experience. There is no need to shame or judge ourselves, as doing so diminishes our brilliant light and reflects a false narrative to the world. Our external reality mirrors what we carry within ourselves.

So, let us not belittle ourselves but embrace our innate creative power. Let us transform our experiences through alchemical change. When we think of alchemy, we envision shifting and transmuting something to a higher level or reality, like turning a simple metal into gold. This occurs when we delve into the depths of our shadow aspects, changing our inner makeup into something greater than before. Just like a diamond that is created under great pressure, our experiences shape us into beautiful gems. This is the alchemical process unfolding on a physiological, emotional, mental, and spiritual level.

I was recently given the image of a butterfly tightly enclosed in its cocoon. The cocoon was dark, rigid, and constricting. Breaking down this rigidity and darkness was the only way to create space for transformation. As the cocoon loosened, the butterfly burst forward, free and vibrant with color. This process of transmutation can also make us rigid and narrow-minded in our beliefs, leaving no room for anything else. However, when an alchemical change occurs or our consciousness shifts, a whole spectrum of colors, expressions, and expansion becomes possible.

This journey holds the beauty of stepping into the transformative process. Each inward journey we embark upon enables us to shift into new levels of consciousness and awareness, releasing the difficulties that obstruct the expression of life's beauty and love. It is during these moments that a simple statement from a wise teacher can have profound and life-changing effects, as we are open to receiving their wisdom.

When we become aware that our inner transformation manifests in our outer reality, the journey becomes exhilarating, bringing miracles into our everyday lives. This journey begins by transforming what we have stored within our lower chakras, where many trauma patterns reside, affecting the energy flow in our upper chakras. The middle path commences in the heart center, where the connection between our spiritual and physical worlds begins.

Our breath serves as the vehicle for bringing new light and energy into the areas that have been dark, tight, and rigid. Simply by breathing and absorbing the vibration of these words, we can facilitate the shift away from rigid behaviors and thoughts. Wisdom and unconditional love, bestowed upon us by the wise sages, facilitate this transformation.

All of us yearn to reach up and experience a profound connection with the Divine Mother and Father within. This connection may be represented by figures such as Mother Mary, Quan Yin, Mother Teresa, Jesus, Buddha, or the Dalai Lama. These powerful teachers show us that by cultivating love and compassion for ourselves, we begin to radiate as we are meant to. As we journey forward, a path of liberation unfolds, which has proven to be a powerful tool for healing in various spiritual traditions. These tools are becoming increasingly accessible in our world as we undergo a significant shift toward higher levels of consciousness. It is time to emerge from the darkness and allow our internal light to shine, expanding our consciousness and reuniting our love, wisdom, science, and spiritual paths to create balance in our world. These aspects were always intended to be together, rather than separate.

Hypnotherapy

Hypnotherapy is an ancient technique that has been utilized by numerous teachers and healers to bring about profound change. It involves bringing our thoughts and beliefs that contribute to suffering into conscious awareness, allowing us to shift our reality and embrace healing and higher ways of being. Unlike temporary energy shifts, hypnotherapy enables us to explore and clear these patterns on a deeper level.

It's important to differentiate between hypnosis and hypnotherapy. Hypnosis primarily utilizes suggestions to induce change, such as in smoking cessation or weight loss programs. Contrary to popular depictions in media, hypnosis cannot make individuals do things they do not want to do. This also applies to the healing aspect, if someone does not genuinely desire to heal, hypnosis will not be effective. Hypnotherapy, on the other hand, delves deeper into therapeutic shifts involving thoughts and beliefs that hypnosis does not specifically target.

Hypnotherapy involves entering a light hypnotic state of relaxation to access the unconscious realms of the mind and uncover the origins of patterns. This state can be compared to moments when we drive from one place to another without conscious recollection or when we drift off to sleep at night. Considering the physiological response to trauma, we know that the mind can become stuck in lower functioning. The brain may not recognize that an event has ended and will continue to respond in the same manner until instructed otherwise. Hypnotherapy can access these stuck points by exploring the most recent time when a negative pattern emerged in our lives.

For instance, let's consider the case of Annie, who seeks therapy due to her ongoing battle with anxiety and depression. She frequently experiences emotional numbness and a loss of direction in her life. Annie occasionally turns to substances like alcohol or marijuana to cope, but she no longer wishes to rely on them.

At this point, it becomes apparent that something is impacting Annie's current life, and there is likely a core issue that needs to be addressed and released. To begin the regression process, I would guide her back to the most recent time she felt anxiety and depression. Annie shares that she feels very alone in her relationship because her husband is always working, leaving her overwhelmed with household responsibilities. She describes having difficulty breathing and experiencing exhaustion and stomach discomfort. As Annie connects with this event, her emotions start to surface.

By activating this stuck portion, we engage the emotional amygdala, which triggers automatic survival responses. This is the point where regression can commence. The purpose of regression is to guide the individual back to the origin of the event, which could be in this lifetime or a past life. Each person has an internal system guided by their higher self that intuitively knows where to take them and which aspects to address first. It is crucial to honor and follow this guidance.

During the session, Annie uncovers that she is ten years old, and her parents have decided to divorce. She concludes that love is not available and does not last, leading her to disconnect from her emotional self to avoid the pain. Consequently, she loses her sense of direction and purpose in life, as her healing ability is embodied by her ten-year-old self. This disconnection not only activates her present-day depression and anxiety but also results in soul fragmentation. When we discard parts of ourselves, we lose the associated gifts and talents. It is vital to reintegrate these fragmented parts to establish a solid energetic field that prevents carrying others' energy and creating illness. Remember that energy cannot be created or destroyed, so when we release a part of ourselves, something else must fill its place.

I find that when someone experiences progress but eventually slips back, it may indicate a need for soul retrieval work. This work is crucial for individuals who have endured significant trauma, as it helps them release what is not theirs and reclaim what is rightfully theirs. Changing old beliefs, thoughts, and behaviors is of utmost importance. In this case, it would involve transforming the belief that love does not last into a more positive affirmation, such as "I am always connected with love and spirit. I am open to receiving love and loving myself." This process involves reclaiming and healing the part of oneself that feels, ultimately fostering more love and creativity in life. Moreover, this process rewires the brain, creating new neural pathways and activating the prefrontal cortex, which expands our options and enhances higher-level thinking.

If we were to conduct another regression, we might delve even deeper into the issue. Perhaps this time, the individual finds themselves in the womb, sensing their mother's depression and anxiety about caring for another baby. As the baby, they have no knowledge beyond the fact that the entire world revolves around them, or that the energy they are experiencing is not their own. This reveals another unconscious pattern they were born with yet remain unaware of. It is evident that years of talk therapy may not uncover such a pattern.

Unfortunately, the baby would be born believing they cause problems for others and love is highly conditional based on their actions. This belief is instinctual and aimed at ensuring survival. It is important to note that babies do not possess language yet, so they process the world differently. However, this does not mean they lack access to these events; they simply need translation into language. This is where the power of hypnotherapy comes into play, bridging the unconscious regions and bringing them to the area of the brain where language and processing can occur, allowing us to understand why we are stuck.

Sometimes, regression can take us to other lifetimes or dimensions where experiences have taken place, and an individual is still seeking correction and learning. In my experience, hypnotherapy has proven to be one of the most potent healing tools available. I have explored various techniques and continue to be amazed by its transformational power. It is an honor to witness the courage and power displayed by each client as they delve into their wounded areas, reclaiming, shifting, and healing aspects of their lives. Witnessing how individuals carry this transformation into their homes, work lives, and personal lives creates a profound shift for humanity as a whole. I cannot fathom quitting this work, as I continually experience powerful changes in my own life through the process.

Hypnotherapy encompasses various techniques, and I have received training in several different styles, each serving its own purpose. When seeking a practitioner, it is crucial to find someone who has personally undergone these sessions in addition to providing them to others. A therapist's understanding of this technique cannot be deepened solely through working on others. Additionally, it is essential to feel a connection and compatibility with the practitioner. The healing space is sacred, and without feeling held and supported, one may not be able to access the depths necessary for healing. Different techniques offer varying levels of depth. Personally, I am drawn to working with deeper techniques such as RoHun and Heart Centered Hypnotherapy, but it is important to follow one's intuition and choose what feels right for them.

Breathwork

Stanislav Grof discusses that in order to create a profound change in consciousness, the breath can be used to access this. Ancient and non-Western cultures have used certain processes to intervene with spiritual aspects to create change in their lives. This can range from subtle to sophisticated exercises. Breathing techniques have been documented in written history for over 4,000 years and have been used as a path to psycho-spiritual development.

In moments of trauma, one of our initial responses is to hold our breath. By not breathing, we inadvertently halt the process of feeling and processing the trauma, causing it to become trapped within our physical, mental, and emotional bodies. Utilizing breathwork can help release this trapped energy, facilitating the flow within our emotional and mental bodies.

If we were to observe a room and identify the person most in control of their emotional and mental state, it would likely be the one who engages in slower and deeper breathing. Conversely, individuals with less control over their emotional and mental states tend to exhibit short, irregular breaths. Incorporating a breathing technique into daily life can greatly benefit those who struggle with anxiety. It is important to note that when using breathwork, the person must be ready to confront and process certain emotions in order to release anxiety.

Anxiety often stems from being disconnected from the present moment and fixating on future "what ifs." Consciously engaging in the act of breathing brings us into the present moment. However, it is essential to use a breathing technique that allows for cathartic release, enabling us to purge and release what is no longer needed.

When we haven't fully processed an experience, our body becomes stuck in a pattern that persists until we direct our breath to facilitate the necessary release. As humans with the capacity for higher thinking through our prefrontal cortex, we often suppress our natural response of releasing what is no longer needed, fearing that it might cause a scene or disrupt our surroundings. This contradicts the innate process of letting go. Observing wild animals, we notice that they allow their bodies to shake and release trauma. As humans, we override this response.

For instance, if we are raised in an environment where having emotions is discouraged and we are taught to cope without expressing them, we may automatically stop breathing to avoid feeling. Pay attention to the next time you experience something stressful or shocking because you may notice a pause in your breath. We even have sayings like "suck it up," "stop being so emotional," or "don't be a baby," which imply the need to suppress emotions, cease processing, and move on.

However, this approach prevents us from returning to process what occurred, and eventually, these unresolved issues will manifest in unexpected ways, reminding us that we still need to confront them. Notably, professions that demand toughness and strength such as police officers, military personnel, or paramedics, often experience high rates of addiction and suicide. This mentality contributes to such correlations.

When I joined the military, I consciously chose to shut down my intuition as it overwhelmed me. I became skilled at suppressing my emotions, numbing myself, and not breathing. Initially, this seemed like an effective solution because I believed I had no control over my sensitivity. In reality, I was building walls and disconnecting myself, leading to increased coldness, anger, and feelings of isolation. It was far from a genuine solution. As I discovered more tools and embraced my sensitivity, I no longer felt disconnected and alone. I can now fully engage in my life.

Circular breathing techniques allow us to connect our mind, body, and spirit. This technique involves conscious, connected breaths through an open mouth, maintaining a continuous flow without pauses. Imagine a circular motion, where inhalation moves up the back and exhalation starts in the front, creating a continuous cycle. Some may describe this breath as noisy, which is accurate because if we cannot hear the breath or if it is not fast enough, it is not conscious, connected breathing. Exhalation should occur naturally, releasing with an "AHH" sound. This breathwork helps us move beyond resistance, surrender, and integrate the changes necessary for expansion and healing. I strongly recommend working with a facilitator who can teach and guide you through this technique.

During a typical breathwork session, we begin by setting an intention. Once the intention is set, we no longer need to focus on it throughout the entire session because the breath itself will do the work. Initially, the breath may bring up resistance, which reflects areas of blockage in our lives. It is important to persist through this initial resistance, as it will eventually pass. If you want to expedite this process, increase the pace of your breathing. The intention you set will bring to the surface the areas that need attention and release.

This could manifest in various ways—physically, mentally, emotionally, or spiritually. It is important to note that each session will be unique and different from the previous ones. The healing aspect of breathwork is incredibly powerful, and while it is impossible to name all its effects, here is a brief list to give you an idea of its potential: detoxification of the body, immune system enhancement, improved digestion, stress reduction, support in creating new neural pathways, increased relaxation and peace, enhanced mental clarity and creativity, deeper intimacy, and strengthened spiritual connections.

Hypnotherapy and breathwork are both techniques that allow us to access the unconscious aspects of ourselves. As you read this, it is essential to understand that your conscious mind is trying to comprehend these concepts. To truly grasp the depth of these techniques, firsthand experience is necessary; it is not enough to simply read about and understand in a cognitive way. It is through this experiential journey that we can bridge the conscious and unconscious aspects of our mind, leading to a deeper understanding of these techniques and ourselves. If you feel that your previous therapy experiences primarily consisted of talking and exploring the conscious aspects, you have only tapped into the 10 percent that is consciously processed. There is still the remaining 90 percent that resides in the unconscious realm, holding the answers to discovering our True Selves.

Chanting

Chanting entered my life when I reached my thirties. Initially, I was uncertain about its purpose and significance. Because of the language, the songs were unfamiliar to me, and I didn't understand the meaning behind them or why I should sing them. However, as I started joining the group in their morning chanting sessions, I noticed profound shifts and changes within my entire being. Chanting had the ability to evoke emotions, instill a deep sense of peace, and even alleviate physical discomforts such as sinus congestion or headaches. Chanting serves as a powerful tool to remove energetic blocks by harnessing the sacred sounds that are incorporated in the practice.

I have always been captivated by a story that was shared about the birthday song. Although it is just a story, it has a powerful message about vibration. I would like to share this beloved tale with you. According to the story, there was a tribe that recognized the unique vibration or frequency of each individual. When a woman in the tribe became aware of her pregnancy, she would venture into the woods and meditate with the unborn child to discern their personal song. The woman would not return to the tribe until she had received this song. Once discovered, she would share it with the tribe, who would learn and sing the song upon the birth of the baby. This sacred song accompanied every significant event in the child's life, and if the child ever felt out of balance, the tribe would surround them and sing the song to realign and restore their authentic essence. Each child's song possessed a specific frequency that facilitated the individual's connection to their True Self.

This tale exemplifies the profound understanding that there is an interconnectedness with us all and our vibration is a powerful tool and the transformative power of sound in realigning and shifting our being when necessary. Our words are also a vibration that can bring us into a higher frequency or lower frequency.

Chanting involves the recognition that when we sing certain tones, we bring our bodies back into alignment with their natural state. The roof of the mouth, like the rest of the body, has interconnected energy channels. It is fascinating how our bodies are designed in such a way that working on one part, such as the feet or the ears, can have a holistic impact on the entire system. "As above, so below; as below, so above." The roof of the mouth contains eighty-two reflex points. Thus, as we engage in sacred chants, we are essentially stimulating and harmonizing these points, restoring balance and vitality. Hindu traditions have long recognized the immense power of this practice, which also activates the vagus nerve discussed earlier, reawakening our social engagement system.

With the availability of various types of music, it is effortless to find talented artists through music streaming platforms. Additionally, kirtan (devotional singing) gatherings are increasingly prevalent in cities nowadays. Engaging in chanting within a group setting amplifies the power of healing and fosters a profound sense of collective energy when approached with respect and reverence.

Meditation

Meditation is a practice that has been extensively researched and proven to offer numerous benefits. Given the wealth of existing information on this topic, I won't delve into it further here. However, in the context of our discussion, daily meditation serves as a valuable tool for realigning with our higher self. By integrating regular moments of meditation throughout our day, we can cultivate a natural inclination toward maintaining a higher vibrational state than our ego-driven tendencies. This state of being expands and supports us, allowing us to access our inner resources.

As we engage in deeper inner work over the years, we can eventually reach a point where meditation becomes a powerful catalyst for positive changes and transformation in our lives.

Core Energetics

Dr. John Pierrakos, MD, is the founder of Core Energetics, an evolutionary therapy that combines body-psychotherapy with spirituality. Core Energetics is rooted in the principles of bioenergetics, but it incorporates the spiritual aspect that was not present in traditional bioenergetics. Dr. Pierrakos believed that patients seek not only healing and relief from past wounds and traumas, but also meaning, purpose, and the authentic expression of their innate qualities in life.

The Core Energetics approach consists of four phases that naturally progress throughout the course of therapy. Although each phase focuses on specific aspects, they can overlap within a single session as the liberation of blocked energy and consciousness takes place. The four phases are penetrating the mask, transforming the lower self, centering in the higher self, and connecting to the universal plan. Each phase encourages a deep exploration of our personality and facilitates a more authentic connection with our essence and the fullness of our energy.

The first phase addresses the superficial layer, known as the mask, which represents the persona we present to the world. It encompasses our personality. The second phase involves transforming our lower self or shadow side. The third phase is centered around connecting with our higher self, which embodies our elevated qualities. The final phase encompasses the deep understanding and experience of our interconnectedness with all aspects of life.

Core Energetics is a profound therapeutic process that goes beyond conventional bodywork or energetic practices. It brings forth hidden aspects of ourselves that may be concealed in other therapeutic modalities, as the body is a truthful reflection of our inner state.

Emotional Freedom Technique (EFT)

Emotional Freedom Technique (sometimes simply referred to as *tapping*) can be utilized individually to address issues that have been keeping us stuck and unable to progress. The premise of tapping is based on the idea that meridians, or energy channels, can become blocked when we experience trauma. Just as the brain can get stuck in patterns, the flow of energy can also become stagnant, reflecting our thoughts and beliefs.

When using EFT, we always begin with a setup statement: "Even though _____, I deeply and completely love and accept myself." For instance, if someone is dealing with feelings of unworthiness, they might say, "Even though I feel unworthy to receive love, I deeply and completely love and accept myself." While tapping on the meridians, this statement is repeated, allowing any emotions or thoughts to surface. As these emerge, we adjust the statement accordingly until we feel a sense of resolution.

If you are interested in learning more about this technique, there are numerous videos available demonstrating different approaches. You'll be amazed by what you discover.

Each modality, including EFT, has its own way of releasing what no longer serves us and realigning us with our authentic selves. Each step taken allows our hearts to expand and fill with the knowledge that we are unique souls with gifts that cannot be replicated. As we release our deepest fears, recognizing that fear will always keep us from embracing our True Selves, we begin to expand and share our light, harmony, and wisdom. Let us remember our essence, stand tall in the truth of who we are and who others are. When we cultivate compassion for ourselves, we can extend that compassion to others. When we love ourselves, we can share that love with others. By combining our knowledge with love, we can impart our wisdom to others. This planet was designed to foster harmony for all, but first, we must find that harmony within ourselves.

As we delve deeper into the shadow aspects of our being, we come to realize that we have all embodied qualities such as the murderer, drug addict, judge, prostitute, seductress, emotional one, manipulator, non-committed individual, and sufferer, among others. We are all interconnected and part of a greater whole. As we recognize our own actions and motivations, we gain an understanding that others also have their unique journeys and reasons for their actions. This doesn't mean we condone self-abuse, but rather expand our perspective and illuminate our light. We begin to embody the qualities we aspire to possess because when we shed what is not truly us, we can comprehend why the angels stand before us, sending us love and support. We understand that there is never a moment when we are alone or unsupported; we simply need to ask, and they will be there. When our hearts are open, everything falls into place. Release the armor, pain, anger, and sadness. Let go of it all and experience the grace of the divine within us. Allow it to expand and embrace the beautiful beings we truly are.

Tapping Your Inner Resources of Presence

Like a fountain that flows deeply within, I am the powerful creator in this realm. My golden light shines brightly and radiates the truth of who I am. I AM and nothing more. I AM. Let this be my truth. I AM.

As we embrace our role as creators of our world, a sense of expansiveness and holding arises. We gaze at the horizon, recognizing that it's time to move horizontally into the realm of the wise soul. By understanding when we dip into our ego and lower state, we can ascend to a different way of existence that encompasses the creative possibilities of love and light. This realm is open to all who seek it, but we must remove the veil of our perceived identities.

This empowered state as creators can profoundly shift our possibilities, allowing miracles to manifest in our world in an exponential manner. The light within us radiates the essence of our being. Each moment presents us with the choice of what we wish to create. Each creation expands either in a positive or negative light, reflecting a higher or lower level of functioning. As an intuitive channel, I have an inner awareness of the worlds around me, yet they are all contained within me.

Empaths, who are highly sensitive individuals, have developed a way of life centered around scanning the external environment for safety. This ability enables them to absorb emotional and mental energies present in their surroundings, whether positive, negative, or neutral. Often, they are unaware of their own needs and feelings, instead relating primarily to the emotions of others. One of the most potent tools for empaths is cultivating presence and adopting the observer role.

When we exist outside of our energetic field and dissociate from our reality, life becomes excessively sensitive and raw. We fragment and disconnect from where we should be. This limited perspective restricts our view. It differs from intuitive guidance or connecting with others, as this process stems from within. By cultivating awareness and presence, we can turn inward and become attuned to our guidance, needs, True Self, and how to maintain that connection. Our True Self is not somewhere external; it resides within us.

The following are tools that can enhance awareness and presence in our own lives. When we are immersed in the lower mind, we often struggle to be fully present with what is occurring. By becoming the observer of our experiences, we gain awareness of subtle nuances and can respond with more love and fulfillment based on what is truly needed.

The following techniques and tools are provided for exploration and enjoyment. They are meant to be observed without judgment. If we find ourselves judging or labeling, then we have strayed from the observer's position. This is not a state of dissociation but rather a state of active presence and observation.

Presence

Presence involves bringing our entire energetic field into focus within the present moment, connected with our True Self. The True Self can observe without judgment, allowing us to perceive different perspectives and solutions in a compassionate and aware manner. To cultivate presence, we must recognize that fragmented coping mechanisms, resulting from traumatic experiences, prevent us from being fully present in our bodies. These coping mechanisms can manifest as relationship difficulties and lead to overwhelming feelings of shutdown, anger, and retreat, often accompanied by substance use or engaging in distracting activities. When we reach this state, life may feel futile, and our purpose may become unclear.

The goal is to gradually expand our ability to be present in our daily lives. By agreeing to be present and observe our moment-to-moment experiences, rather than focusing on what comes next, what we must do, or what we should say to others, we open ourselves up to the unfolding of fuller expressions of our authentic selves. True miracles occur when we are fully present in the moment.

While there is already ample information available about being empathic, it is my intention to offer a different perspective and expand upon existing knowledge. The aim is to embrace the essence of our being, allowing us to see through the illusions of our previous perceptions without judgment and to release the stagnant patterns holding us back. Being sensitive should not lead to an inability to function in the world due to overwhelm. Instead, being sensitive should enable us to love deeply and experience the profound impact of love when shared and received. From this space, we become open to solutions that benefit all of humanity.

Embracing this experience does not involve shutting down but rather being present enough to compassionately observe and find higher solutions that uplift our patterns. The sacral chakra houses our inner child, which possesses the power to create in divine and magnificent ways. When aligned, this creative energy allows our visionary self to guide the emotional aspect toward higher expressions. If we remain stuck in anxiety, guilt, shame, and fear, our creative expression becomes one that no one enjoys, creating dissonance within ourselves and leading us to absorb the feelings of others. However, it should not be this way.

When we assume the observer role, we open ourselves to witnessing the thoughts, behaviors, and emotions of our inner parts. Through observation, we create space to reflect on what is happening within us. It is through observation that we can initiate change, as we must first become aware of what needs to change. Without awareness, it is like running in the shadows and creating a life based on an unconscious perspective. We cannot transform what we are not conscious of.

Grounding

Grounding is the process of fully embodying ourselves and developing the ability to be present with our internal experiences. There are various ways to ground ourselves, depending on our internal state. By exploring our chakra system and the elements associated with it, we can gain deeper insight into the specific grounding practices that would benefit our physical body.

During my training in Ayurvedic medicine, I recall the teacher explaining how the elements manifest in the body and how to restore balance. As beginners, we all sought a simple answer or formula to achieve balance. However, each individual is unique, and what works for one person may not work the same way for another, even when facing similar challenges. Although each chakra is associated with a specific element, these elements are present throughout the body, constantly interacting with one another. It's like a chess game where we must be aware of the ongoing dynamics and choose the appropriate element to ground ourselves. While we may arrive at a state of ungroundedness and imbalance, the paths we take to get there differ. Therefore, intuitive awareness is essential in determining the specific element that will support our system.

When we consider the earth element, it serves as the anchor that grounds us to this physical plane. It grants us presence in the world. If we find ourselves ungrounded or resistant to being present with something, we can seek practices that facilitate grounding. This may involve connecting with the earth by placing our feet on the ground, utilizing grounding crystals, or engaging with nature. Some individuals find clay masks applied to specific areas of the body to be grounding. Personally, I find using a bio mat with grounding crystals to be beneficial. Additionally, many people wear jewelry with grounding properties to support their presence and grounding.

Crystals have experienced a significant resurgence of interest in recent years. There are encyclopedias dedicated to crystals and their metaphysical properties. Certain crystals, such as obsidian, hematite, tiger's eye, black tourmaline, malachite, and amethyst, are particularly effective for grounding and protection. Black obsidian, for example, is known for its grounding properties. If you tend to resist grounding, carrying a piece of black obsidian in your pocket can help you observe any shifts it brings. Black hematite strengthens the aura and deflects negative energy, connecting with the root chakra. Tiger's eye expands intuition and provides protection. Black tourmaline protects against negative energy. Malachite helps clear emotional blockages, especially during stressful times, promoting calmness and emotional balance. Last, amethyst, one of my personal favorites, facilitates spiritual connection, although its effects can vary among individuals.

If you are new to working with crystals, I can provide a basic introduction on how to clear and use them. When selecting a crystal, the best approach is to choose the one that resonates with you intuitively. Some individuals run their hands over the crystals to sense their vibrations, while others simply know which one is right for them upon sight. Once you have chosen a crystal, it is important to clear it of any energies it may have absorbed, similar to how we cleanse ourselves. Like us, crystals are energetically sensitive and can pick up the energies of their surroundings.

The simplest way to clear a crystal is by running it under water for about ten minutes or until it feels energetically cleansed. During this process, set the intention that the water is purifying the crystal from any previous energies it may have held. However, please note that some crystals should not be placed in water, as they may dissolve. After clearing the crystal, activate it with your intention. In the context of grounding, hold the crystal in your hand and focus your intention on grounding. Feel the purpose infuse into the crystal until you sense that the programming has been set. You may experience a settling sensation in your hand or simply know that the intention has been established. To charge the crystals, you can place them under the moon or sunlight, preferably during a full moon. It is important to note that amethysts should not be exposed to direct sunlight, as they may fade irreversibly.

As we explore the earth element and work with grounding practices, take note of how it feels within your body. Heightened awareness will allow you to recognize when the earth element is out of balance and guide you in restoring that balance.

The water element is closely connected to our emotions, as feeling is essential for the process of creation. If we have been conditioned to believe that only certain emotions are good while others are bad, we disconnect from those "unacceptable" feelings, leading to stagnation and a dull reality. However, this does not mean that our emotions should govern our world and create chaos. Instead, awareness of our feelings allows us to identify what is happening within us and make the necessary changes to bring aliveness and happiness. Without acknowledging and exploring our emotions, we cannot effectively create change. The water element within us serves as a vast center for creation, initiating through the act of feeling. Once we allow ourselves to feel, these emotions can be elevated to the heart and expressed in a loving and illuminated way. When we avoid feeling, we create in the shadows of life, continually receiving shadow energy until we recognize that we are the source of it. The inner child within us acts as both the feeler and the healer. To effectively manifest our visionary ideas held within the third eye, we must reconnect with our ability to feel. Otherwise, we disconnect from our spirit and develop a false belief that our higher source is absent.

When experiencing an imbalance with the water element, we can engage in activities that help restore equilibrium. Taking a bath, drinking cold and hot water, or going for a swim are some effective ways to balance this element. It's important to explore what works best for you personally. You can also incorporate aromatherapy spritzers with oils that resonate with you. The lymphatic system, which is connected to the water element, requires movement to remain active, as it does not move on its own. One effective method is using a rebounder, which helps stimulate lymphatic flow and prevents stagnation. When water becomes too dense, we need something to encourage its movement. Tune inwards to understand what your body needs in terms of balancing the water element.

The fire element plays a vital role in either bringing something into our system or transforming or releasing it. It can ignite passion but can also change into anger. Often, the fire element is used to keep emotions under control, creating a mental rather than deeply felt experience. This may manifest as apprehension, bleakness, or a sense of futility. When the fire element is imbalanced, a lack of vitality is felt, and we may find ourselves going through the motions of daily life without truly experiencing anything. This is where our achiever aspect resides. When we find ourselves merely completing tasks on a to-do list, it indicates an imbalance in both the water and fire elements, hindering our ability to create effectively.

The fire element can be harnessed to burn and release what no longer serves us, as well as to manifest our desires. The key lies in clarity of intention. Spending time in the sun can help rebalance this energy. Focusing on the breath through the right nostril, which is connected to the fire element and SNS, can also bring balance. The practice of pranayama (breathwork) can help restore balance to both sides of the ANS, depending on what is needed. Explore different techniques and practices that resonate with your body's needs to restore balance with the fire element.

The air element is associated with the opening of our hearts and acts as a bridge between the upper and lower chakras. When we can freely think and feel without limitations, we can move into the heart center and experience unconditional love. This element supports our connectedness with others in a loving and compassionate way.

Our thoughts can either bring us closer to the light, allowing us to move vertically toward spirit, or lead us into shadow, where our creations originate.

Balancing the air element can be achieved through breath and sound practices. Engaging in breath exercises, singing, or chanting can be effective in restoring equilibrium. You may discover a sacred chant that resonates with what you seek to balance. Different breathing techniques are available depending on your system's needs. Once again, turn inward to determine what your body requires in terms of the air element.

The breath can be employed in various ways depending on the specific breathwork technique used. The person who has control over their breath has control over the room. When we find ourselves taking short and shallow breaths, it often signifies anxiety, anger, or a lack of control over the situation. Such states can lead to poor decision-making, only realized in hindsight.

By incorporating breathing exercises into our daily lives, we develop the habit of automatically remembering to breathe when faced with stressful situations. Breathwork brings balance to our system. I encourage you to embark on a thirty-day challenge, selecting a specific breath exercise and setting an intention for what you wish to achieve. During the practice, focus on this intention, as concentrated breathing accelerates the manifestation of our desired outcomes in life.

By attuning to the breath, we can cultivate sustained focus on our intention. For instance, let's explore the seven-seven-seven breath. If our intention is abundance, we would inhale for a count of seven, hold the breath for seven counts while solely focusing on abundance, and then exhale for seven counts. This powerful practice can work miracles in our lives. Personally, I have integrated this breathwork throughout my day, finding opportune moments to engage in it. Whether I am running errands in the car, taking a shower, or cleaning, there are endless opportunities to incorporate this breathwork. Remember, inhalation is what we give to ourselves, while exhalation is what we give to the world. (If you are new to breathwork, practicing while driving or in water is not recommended. See your healthcare provider before starting if you have lung/breathing issues.)

Observing changes in our breath can offer valuable insights. If we notice that our focus on the intention wavers, it's important to pause, even if it's only been a minute. This process is designed to enhance focus and presence. When our attention starts to drift, we are inadvertently training ourselves to become distracted. Take your time and observe as you gradually increase your threshold for sustained focus.

Additionally, minerals play a significant role in our system, often unnoticed but necessary for grounding and presence. Consider checking if there are any specific minerals your body may require to restore balance.

As we delve deeper, we discover that different elements may be required for different issues. For example, if we're feeling unwell and experiencing low energy, we can take a moment to identify the underlying cause of this imbalance. It could be that the fire element has been overpowering our emotional energy due to fear of creating chaos in our lives. The fire element often encompasses our young adult energy, while the water element embodies our inner child's desire for emotional expression, which is hindered by the dominance of fire.

In this scenario, taking a bath and allowing ourselves to feel can be beneficial. Once we reconnect with our emotions, we can move forward and create what we desire. However, another individual may require a different approach. Perhaps their absence of the earth element stems from a shocking experience that caused them to disconnect. They may exhibit a lack of emotions, feeling like a zombie going through life. In such a case, using the earth element can help reignite the other elements and restore balance. On the other hand, someone who is overwhelmed by their emotions and has experienced destructive outcomes may need the air element combined with some grounding through earth. It's important not to overthink the process. Each experience with the elements serves as an opportunity to expand our awareness of what we require for grounding and balance.

Elemental Meditations

In this process, we will begin by meditating on each element present within our bodies. We will focus on one element at a time and turn our attention inward to discern its sensations. What does this element feel like to us? Where do we find it in balance? Where is it out of balance? What messages does it have for us? How have we misused this energy in the past? And how can we begin to utilize this energy with integrity? It is crucial to dedicate sufficient time to each element until we can genuinely comprehend the insights it provides. Some elements may require more time than others, and the pace may vary.

Once we have progressed through this exploration of the elements within us, we can shift our awareness to the elements in nature that surround us. We can pose the same questions to these external elements as we did to the internal ones. Each element in nature will exhibit unique characteristics. Some elements may require more time and effort to connect with, while others may feel more familiar and comfortable. These experiences offer valuable insights into our internal landscape and our creative abilities in the world. Given the current state of affairs, it is an opportune time to attune ourselves to the elements and witness the discoveries they unveil. As we move through each element (fire, earth, water, and air), we will enhance our ability to manifest effectively in our lives. When we learn to utilize the elements in harmony, our creative capacities flourish. Conversely, if we misuse the elements, our ability to create is hindered. We need only observe nature itself to understand the impact of uncontrolled fire, excessive water, insufficient air, or hardened earth.

Enjoy the process and embrace the sense of wonder and exploration. You will be astounded by the revelations about yourself and how you shape your world.

Following Inner Sensations

This is a simple exercise that assists us tuning into the body without becoming overwhelmed by thoughts and emotions. It creates a sense of safety and presence within. To begin, enter a light meditative state and observe the sensations in your body. Approach this space with nonjudgment, simply noticing the sensations that arise and focusing on them. It is common for sensations to shift as you direct your attention to them, and you may find yourself drawn to new sensations.

If at any point during the exercise intense emotions arise, gently step out of the process and take some deep breaths. If you feel comfortable, you can return to the exercise later. However, if needed, it's perfectly acceptable to take a break for the day. With continued practice, you will cultivate a greater sense of presence. This exercise also reveals that the sensations you focus on are transient and subject to change. This realization can extend to overwhelming experiences in your external world as well. By identifying sensations, you can discern what belongs to you and what does not. This awareness allows you to release sensations, feelings, or thoughts that were never yours to begin with.

Eye Gazing

Eye gazing is a practice that allows you to explore the different aspects of your being. Each eye represents distinct qualities. The left eye serves as the gateway to the soul, while the right eye reflects your outward personality.

To engage in this process, set aside a few minutes each day to gaze into your own eyes. Direct your focus solely on your eyes, excluding distractions like your hair or surroundings. As you observe your eyes, pay attention to any changes or shifts that occur. You may notice variations in brightness, moments of light and dullness, or the emergence of shadow aspects. You might also gain insight into different parts of yourself and their influence on your life. Remember, the purpose of this exercise is not to judge these aspects but to bring awareness to them. By consciously acknowledging these parts, you can make intentional shifts in your behavior if necessary, moving toward a more positive expression of self.

Heart Center

The heart center is a powerful tool for grounding and centering ourselves. By placing your hand on your heart, you can tune into the energy residing there. As you connect with your heart, you can also say affirmations like "Here I am," reaffirming your presence and grounding in the present moment. This simple practice helps you reestablish your balance and flow. Whenever you encounter something shocking or feel disconnected, you can pause, take a deep breath, and direct your focus to your heart. Breathing into your heart center activates your essence and allows the energy to flow once again.

To deepen this exercise, you can incorporate movement. Turning in the four directions, take a step forward with your right foot and declare, "I am here." This action invites any scattered or fragmented energy to return, ensuring that you feel fully present. As you engage in this process, you'll notice an enhanced sense of presence and groundedness.

Black and White Stones

This process aims to cultivate presence and observation in daily life. The goal is to observe experiences without labeling them as good or bad, but simply being present with them.

To begin, visit a craft store and obtain a bag of black and white stones. These stones will be used to represent the events of the day. As you move through your day, select a stone that corresponds to each event or interaction. For example, if you wake up feeling excited and engage in a heartwarming interaction with your dog, choose a white stone. Conversely, if a coworker says something that triggers anger within, select a black stone. Continue this process, picking stones that reflect the nature of each event, until the day comes to an end.

Once you have completed this exercise, take a moment to observe the bowl filled with stones, representing your day's experiences. It allows you to see where you are operating from the perspective of an observer, detached from the ego's judgments and entanglements. By practicing non-judgmental observation, you transcend the influence of the ego.

After finishing the process, return the stones to their original place. Then, take several deep breaths, intentionally releasing the energy of the day, allowing it to dissolve. This helps to fully let go of the day's energy and prepares you for a fresh start.

True Self Meditation

The following is a meditation that will help you connect with your True Self, the part of you that holds the cosmic DNA of your True Spirit and understands your path and the bigger picture. By recording this meditation and listening to it, you can deepen your connection with your True Self.

To begin, find a comfortable position and take several deep breaths, allowing yourself to settle and adjust your body. With each breath, feel a sense of relaxation washing over you, releasing tension from your muscles and calming your mind. If your mind starts to wander, gently bring your focus back to the breath. Within the breath resides your spirit, so follow its rhythm as it moves in and out, allowing yourself to become increasingly relaxed.

As you relax, visualize yourself standing on a beautiful path. Feel the warmth of the sun on your face as you become aware of your feet on the path. The path leads you up a majestic mountain, and with each step, you feel lighter and freer. Notice your molecules and cells shifting as you ascend. As you climb higher, you encounter a radiant green light energy. Take a moment to connect with this light and feel its essence. Now, breathe this light into every cell and molecule of your body, allowing it to permeate your being.

As you continue along the path, it gently twists and curves. The energy of the light changes, transforming into a soothing light blue color. This light blue fills your mind and heart, awakening your inner wisdom. Feel this inner wisdom stirring within you. Breathe it into any areas that need it, taking all the time you need in this space before proceeding along the path.

Moving onward, lighter and freer, you ascend the majestic mountain, experiencing its unique energy. This energy brings a profound sense of connectedness and deep peace, transcending the struggles of earthly existence. You feel a lightness as the luminous energy recalibrates your entire system, enveloping you in golden light. Allow yourself to remember and embody your true essence, repeating the affirmation "I am. I am. I am. I am. I am the light. Feel the light. I am. I am."

In your hand, you now hold a wand of light, a divine gift. As you gently brush it in front of your eyes, you feel the veils lifting, allowing clarity and insight. Brush the wand over your ears, clearing any blockages and opening yourself to hearing truth. Let the golden light from the wand flow into your eyes and ears, filling those spaces. With each breath, create a beautiful field of golden light around you, acknowledging that you *are* this light.

As you immerse yourself in the love of this light, allow it to flow through your entire being. Feel yourself merging with this love and light, knowing that you are one with it.

Continuing on your journey, you reach the summit of the mountain, taking in the breathtaking scenery. The colors of the flowers, trees, and water radiate with luminosity. In the distance, you notice a magnificent temple, a place that resonates deeply with your heart and soul. Approach the temple, hearing beautiful sounds emanating from within. As you open the doors, absorb the surroundings, and inquire about the purpose of the symbols present, seeking insights into your spiritual path.

Through a doorway, a being emerges—an embodiment of pure love. As you gaze into their eyes, you realize this being is your True Self. Your True Self takes your hand and touches it to your heart, allowing loving energy to flow through you. They then touch your third eye, awakening the energy of love within this center of wisdom. The True Self affirms that you are one, containing your True Spiritual DNA and the wisdom of the ages. Breathe in this connection and say yes to merging with your True Self. Feel the energy flowing through the crown of your head, and with each breath, allow it to fill your entire body.

When the merging process feels complete, you notice a beautiful chair nearby. Sit on this chair and open yourself to receiving any messages pertaining to your current path. Take your time in this space.

Now, gently and in your own time, begin to move back down the path. With each step, feel yourself fully returning to your body, reintegrating the energy that has shifted within you. Take a few moments to settle, and when you're ready, gradually open your eyes, feeling alive, aware, and awake.

Bringing the Light into the World

Oh, my soul. My heart cries out to remember who I am. It is the eternal flow of love that sounds and vibrates within me. Please show me the way. Show me the way back to you. There is a gentle light that I feel and see, is that the way? My heart reminds me to open and feel and to let go of the darkness; it is not you. Yet, surrounded by the darkness it is hard to see. Within that darkness, a light sparks. The energy of the light says to remember who you are! You are a part of God's light. Bring forth that part which you have chosen to share. Give that with an open heart and with love and also with an open mind, with wisdom. Feel the truth of who you are and go out into the world.

As a child, I remember the feeling of boundless possibilities and a deep sense of love and connection with everything around me. However, as I grew older, I became aware that the world didn't always share this perspective. I encountered cruelty and began to question the idea of love in a world that seemed harsh. In response, I started looking outside myself for answers, distancing myself from my inner truth and losing sight of my purpose.

Throughout this journey, we have learned that we are all interconnected and contribute to the collective consciousness. Our contributions can either enhance our planet or create unnecessary challenges. It is our responsibility to examine ourselves and make amends, correcting our course of action. Each of us has a unique purpose, but when unconscious beliefs and emotions take control, we become stuck in negative patterns.

In our realities, there are no true victims because we are the creators of our experiences. We have the power to change this. We are spiritual beings who have forgotten our connection to God and the choice to create from our higher purpose or our lower ego. To truly know ourselves, we must explore our conscious, super-conscious, and unconscious parts, including our shadow, trickster, and victim triangle. Understanding that we all possess these aspects and have experienced them in this or previous lifetimes allows us to recognize them in others. What we dislike in others is sometimes a reflection of what we also carry within ourselves. As my teacher would say, "if you can spot it, you got it."

Why is this understanding so crucial? Our world is undergoing a shift, and we all play a role in how this transformation unfolds. An invisible grid surrounds our planet, holding the energies we collectively contribute. When we turn to the media, we witness the destruction of our planet through natural disasters, governmental struggles, and family divisions driven by the need to be right. Mother Earth is responding to our aggressive behaviors with fires, floods, and hurricanes. We contribute to this through our unaware behaviors, beliefs, and decisions. If we are unwilling to explore the unknown aspects within ourselves, how can we hope to understand and change our external reality? Our personal lives cannot transform, and the collective consciousness cannot elevate without this introspection. It only takes a small percentage of the population, approximately 9 percent, to initiate a significant shift.

I often reflect on my time in the Navy, where the prevailing message was to suppress emotions and move forward. However, I have come to realize that this approach is pushing us farther from our truth. When we refuse to address our internal issues, we often turn to unhealthy coping mechanisms, leading to high rates of suicide and addiction among military personnel. True strength comes from acknowledging that something is not working and venturing into the unknown for deeper healing. Many individuals are awakening to the realization that this approach no longer serves them, and they seek to reconnect with their higher purpose and reclaim their sense of aliveness.

The good news is that we don't need the entire world to embark on this journey. A small portion of the population can be the pioneers of our new world, which lies within us. As we embark on the inward journey of healing, we unlock new possibilities that we never thought possible. Just like elephants clearing a path for others, we can pave the way with our understanding of who we are and how we transcend our current circumstances. This is a journey for the brave because, like explorers, we often don't know what to expect. However, with each step, we discover a deeper well of compassion, love, and light within us. From this space, we gain a profound understanding of the importance of avoiding bringing harm to others and the power of our creations to make shifts within and beyond ourselves.

As the physiological response has shown us, we have the ability to rewire our system and change our responses. However, in order to do so, we must be willing to delve into the darkness and address what is holding us back. By understanding how our beliefs and behaviors were formed (often rooted in fear), we can then rewire and transform these patterns. This process creates space for love, harmony, wisdom, laughter, peace, and a better world to flourish. Embrace this transformation like a peaceful warrior, relinquishing the sword of destruction and embracing the sword of light. Allow your inner light to shine as a beacon of serenity and hope for the future.

In the years to come, we will discover more sacred teachings that were once lost. We will turn inward, not out of selfishness, but because everything we need resides within us. There will be opportunities to redefine ourselves as individuals and communities, supporting one another in a loving and empowering manner rather than living in codependency. Each of us has a unique path and soul journey, and what resonates with one person may not resonate with another. This diversity is essential for learning and growth. The beautiful tapestry of our collective consciousness is woven together by the unique vibrations radiating from each individual.

Rise and let your heart resonate with your distinct frequency that makes you an extraordinary, once-in-a-lifetime experience. Embrace this step, knowing it will be the most exhilarating journey you have ever embarked upon.

I had the privilege of conducting holistic care research on a palliative care floor at a hospital years ago. During this time, I had the honor of sitting with individuals as they prepared to transition from this physical realm into their energetic essence. It became clear that those aware of their limited time never spoke about meeting everyone's expectations or working harder. Their reflections centered on missed opportunities and the realization that they could never reclaim those moments. They longed for more love, connection, sharing, and creativity. Not once did I hear anyone say, "I wish I had worked more." The wisdom lies in living each day as if it were our last. How would this change our actions? Would we have the courage to follow our hearts' desires? Can we release the belief that control over everything ensures happiness? And can we let go of the fear that love does not exist and understand how this belief was formed?

Another profound lesson I learned during this research was the rapid dissolution of barriers for many individuals. There was a realization that certain matters needed to be attended to. I remember one patient who grappled with their belief in God and the existence of anything beyond this life—a true existential crisis. This person knew their time was running out. Books on different religions and beliefs lined their bed tray. We engaged in conversations, but mostly I listened.

During this period, I also conducted energetic body sessions with patients. One night, while I was asleep, this patient appeared in my dreams, confused, and seeking guidance on where to go. I spent the night leading them to the light that always awaits. I'm uncertain if our discussions made a difference, but they found their way home, connecting with me on the astral plane. Somehow, we always find our way home. We may occasionally feel lost, but the light is ever-present. When we are committed to uncovering the truth of who we are, even when it seems like nothing is there, I assure you, you will always find your light, your True Self.

This is the process of alchemy of the soul.

Reading List

Alice A. Bailey books

Autobiography of a Yogi, Paramahansa Yogananda

Becoming Supernatural, Dr. Joe Dispenza

Bioenergetics, Alexander Lowen, M.D.

Breaking Free from the Victim Trap, Diane Zimberoff

Core Energetics, John C. Pierrakos, M.D.

Emotional Anatomy, Stanley Keleman

God as Divine Mother, Paramhansa Yogananda and Swami Kriyananda

Healing of Light, Barbara Ann Brennan

Inner Work: Using Dreams and Active Imagination for Personal Growth, Robert A. Johnson

It Didn't Start With You, Mark Wolynn

Journeys into the Heart, Drunvalo Melchizedek and Daniel Mitel

Light Emerging, Barbara Ann Brennan

Living in the Heart, Drunvalo Melchizedek

Man and His Symbols, Carl Jung

Our Polyvagal World: How Safety and Trauma Change Us, Stephen Porges, Ph.D

Overcoming Shock, Diane Zimberoff and David Hartmann

Polyvagal Exercises for Safety and Connection, Deb Dana

Revelations of Christ, Paramhansa Yogananda

Spiritual Emergency, Stanislov Grof

The Adventure of Self-Discovery, Stanislov Grof

The Body Keeps Score, Bessel Van der Kolk, Ph.D

The Essence of the Bhagavad Gita, Paramhansa Yogananda

The Four Agreements, Don Miguel Ruiz

The Gene Keys, Richard Rudd

The Holotropic Mind, Stanislov Grof

The Invisible Garment, Connie Kaplan
The Kybalion, Three Initiates
The Oversoul Seven Trilogy, Jane Roberts
The Quantum Human, Karen Curry Parker
The Undefended Self, Susan Thesenga
Understanding Human Design, Karen Curry Parker
Understanding the Centers in Human Design, Robin Winn, MFT
Waking the Tiger: Healing Trauma, Peter Levine, Ph.D
Wheels of Life, Anodea Judith, Ph.D

Bibliography

American Psychiatric Association. *DSM-5 Handbook of Differential Diagnosis.* Washington D.C.: American Psychiatric Publishing, 2014.

Dana, Deb. *The Polyvagal Theory in Therapy: Engaging the Rhythm of Regulation.* W.W. Norton & Company, 2018.

Grof, Stanislav. *Healing Our Deepest Wounds: The Holotropic Paradigm Shift.* Stream of Experience Productions, 2012.

Jung, C. G. 1875-1961, Man and His Symbols. Garden City, N.Y., Anchor Books/Doubleday, 1964.

Ogden, P. Sensorimotor Psychotherapy. W.W. Norton & Company Ltd., 2015.

Porges, S. W. *The Polyvagal Theory: Neurophysiological Foundations of Emotions, Attachment, Communication, and Self-Regulation.* New York: W.W. Norton & Company, 2011.

Parker, Karen Curry. Quantum Human Design Coach Mastermind Training Program, 2021.

Krippner, Stanley, and Deirdre Barrett. "Transgenerational Trauma: The Role of Epigenetics." *The Journal of Mind and Behavior* 40, no. 1 (Winter 2019): 53–62. https://www.jstor.org/stable/26740747.

Welwood, Heart-Centered Hypnotherapy training handout, 1990.

Yehuda, Rachel and Amy Lehrner. "Intergenerational transmission of trauma effects: putative role of epigenetic mechanisms." *World Psychiatry* 17, no. 3 (Oct. 2018):243-257. https://www.wpanet.org/_files/ugd/e172f3_b4d1f99a589a496b88f4d27234b09674.pdf

About the Author

Sarah Lahoski is a licensed professional clinical counselor with a rich educational background from the University of Akron. As a transpersonal hypnotherapist and holistic health practitioner, she has studied Ayurvedic medicine and various energy healing modalities. Additionally, Sarah serves as a spiritual coach and teacher, dedicated to exploring the possibilities within the world and infusing that same enthusiasm into her work with clients.

She is the owner of Transformative Path, where she specializes in guiding empaths and intuitives through the process of removing blocks and traumas that hinder access to their innate gifts. Sarah envisions a world where individual healing and release lead to positive changes in families and communities, fostering greater love, unity, and profound connections. She believes these transformations can create new ways of impacting the world.

With over seventeen years of professional experience in her spiritual journey, Sarah is passionate about fostering deep, meaningful connections. She values mutual learning and growth, and her lighthearted approach to life is reflected in her interactions with clients, friends, and loved ones. Known for her unique ability to create personalized songs—though she humbly admits they're not always perfect—Sarah also enjoys crafting intuitive art, immersing herself in nature, expanding consciousness, and cherishing time with her loved ones.

www.sarahlahoski.com
www.transformativepath.com

For more great books from The Empower Press
Visit Books.GracePointPublishing.com

PEAK PRESS

If you enjoyed reading *Alchemy of the Soul,* and purchased it through an online retailer, please return to the site and write a review to help others find the book.

Printed in the USA
CPSIA information can be obtained
at www.ICGtesting.com
LVHW010622011224
797923LV00015B/660